How to teach modern languages – and survive!

MODERN LANGUAGES IN PRACTICE
Series Editor: Michael Grenfell, *Centre for Language in Education, University of Southampton.*
Editorial Board: Do Coyle, *School of Education, University of Nottingham* and Simon Green, *Trinity & All Saints College, Leeds.*
Editorial Consultant: Christopher Brumfit, *Centre for Language in Education, University of Southampton.*

The Modern Languages in Practice Series provides publications on the theory and practice of modern foreign language teaching. The theoretical and practical discussions in the publications arise from, and are related to, research into the subject. *Practical* is defined as having pedagogic value. *Theoretical* is defined as illuminating and/or generating issues pertinent to the practical. Theory and practice are, however, understood as a continuum. The series includes books at three distinct points along this continuum: (1) Limited discussions of language learning issues. These publications provide an outlet for coverage of actual classroom activities and exercises. (2) Aspects of both theory and practice combined in broadly equal amounts. This is *the core of the series*, and books may appear in the form of collections bringing together writers from different fields. (3) More theoretical books examining key research ideas directly relevant to the teaching of modern languages.

Some Other Books in the Series
Effective Language Learning
    Suzanne Graham
The Elements of Foreign Language Teaching
    Walter Grauberg
Fluency and its Teaching
    Marie-Noelle Guillot
Foreign Language and Culture Learning from a Dialogic Perspective
    Carol Morgan and Albane Cain
French Words: Past, Present and Future
    Malcolm Offord
The Good Language Learner
    N. Naiman, M. Fröhlich, H.H. Stern and A. Todesco
Inspiring Innovations in Language Teaching
    Judith Hamilton
Language Learners as Ethnographers
    Celia Roberts, Michael Byram, Ana Barro, Shirley Jordan and Brian Street
Le ou La? The Gender of French Nouns
    Marie Surridge
Motivating Language Learners
    Gary N. Chambers
New Perspectives on Teaching and Learning Modern Languages
    Simon Green (ed.)
Switched on? Video Resources in Modern Language Settings
    Steven Fawkes
Target Language, Collaborative Learning and Autonomy
    Ernesto Macaro
Training Teachers in Practice
    Michael Grenfell

Please contact us for the latest book information:
Multilingual Matters, Frankfurt Lodge, Clevedon Hall,
Victoria Road, Clevedon, BS21 7HH, England
http://www.multilingual-matters.com

MODERN LANGUAGES IN PRACTICE 17
Series Editor: Michael Grenfell

How to teach modern languages – and survive!

Jan Pleuger

MULTILINGUAL MATTERS LTD
Clevedon • Buffalo • Toronto • Sydney

To Gilbert, who inspired me,
Maggie Léglise, Christian Lhoumeau and Juan

Library of Congress Cataloging in Publication Data
Pleuger, Jan
How to Teach Modern Languages – And Survive!/Jan Pleuger
Modern Languages in Practice: 17
Includes bibliographical references
1. Languages, Modern–Study and teaching. I. Title. II. Series.
PB35.P54 2001
418′.0071–dc21   2001032704

British Library Cataloguing in Publication Data
A catalogue entry for this book is available from the British Library.

ISBN 1-85359-543-8 (hbk)
ISBN 1-85359-542-X (pbk)

Multilingual Matters Ltd
UK: Frankfurt Lodge, Clevedon Hall, Victoria Road, Clevedon BS21 7HH.
USA: UTP, 2250 Military Road, Tonawanda, NY 14150, USA.
Canada: UTP, 5201 Dufferin Street, North York, Ontario M3H 5T8, Canada.
Australia: Footprint Books, PO Box 418, Church Point, NSW 2103, Australia.

Printed and bound in Great Britain by the Cromwell Press Ltd.

Contents

Acknowledgements

I would like to thank the following for their kind permission to reproduce the illustrations that appear in this book:

Harley-Davidson Europe for the advertisement on page 29.

France Telecom for the advertisement on page 154.

The Nuffield Foundation for the various cartoons throughout the book.

Every effort has been made to trace ownership of all the cartoons, but the publishers would be happy to make arrangements with any copyright holder whom it has not been possible to contact.

Introduction

This is not a book for the teacher of 'high-flyers'. Teaching them languages could not be easier. It is for the teacher of average pupils of any age, but especially those working in large classes in ordinary state schools. I have written mainly about Key Stage 3 and 4, with a nod to A-level here and there, but most of these ideas can be applied to learners at any stage, including adults. For simplicity I have used French as my example, but of course such methods can be used to teach any language.

These practical strategies are aimed principally at reducing both pupil and teacher anxiety. (The two are, of course, closely linked.) They were laboriously arrived at by me, during a long career in modern language teaching, spanning the whole revolution which took place in the last 20 years – the introduction of 'a foreign language for all' (trauma), 'mixed ability language teaching' (more trauma), and the arrival of the National Curriculum (almost terminal trauma). They may not work for you.

The last twenty years has been an exciting time in the language teaching profession. Once upon a time, long ago, it was a tranquil affair, involving only the most academic and well-motivated pupils, who would work industriously on long lists of dry vocabulary and intrinsically meaningless grammar exercises. All this had to change, and it did. With the advent of 'a language for all' (pupils no longer allowed to vote with their feet at age fourteen), we had to turn our attention for the first time to 'motivation'. There was no alternative. A few years later, in came 'mixed ability languages' (no setting), which concentrated our minds on new methods once again: this time it was 'differentiation'. We coped. The final trauma was the introduction of the famous National Curriculum (mountains of paperwork, assessment and centralisation), which, struggle as we might, could only mitigate against both our recent allies, 'motivation' and 'differentiation' (not to mention teachers' free time).

We rose to these challenges magnificently, calling on the many resources of modern technology which for the first time became available to us. We were buffeted by the winds of constant change and the flurry of meetings with county advisors. Courses became a way of life. We re-thought our philosophy over and over again to suit the latest trends. But we battled through. The examination system was re-modelled, our teaching methods were transformed and our classrooms became friendlier and more motivating places.

There remains doubt, however, about the success of foreign language teaching in this country. As our ties with Europe grow stronger, why do so many students give up languages at sixteen? Why do A-level entries decline, and degree courses have fewer applicants? This despite statistics in 1999 showing that modern language graduates have lower unemployment rates than all others, including Maths and Science.[1] A glimmer of hope has appeared on the horizon following the increase in numbers opting to study languages post-16, after the introduction of the 4–5 subject AS level in the year 2000. But, of those who do graduate, fewer are choosing teaching as a career, and large PGCE cash bonuses have had to be introduced by the government in order to entice students of shortage subjects into teaching. What does all this imply for the future of modern languages in our schools?

There are many possible reasons for Britain's lamentable performance in foreign language learning. The growing importance of English as a world language and on the Internet may have lead to feelings of complacency, and the dominance of US culture around the world poses no challenge to us linguistically. The global popularity of a largely English-speaking entertainment industry has motivated young people abroad to learn English, whilst native speakers have no such incentive to learn European languages. Our students are also at a disadvantage in the priority given to foreign languages in our school system. Most schoolchildren in Europe begin learning English sooner, and devote more hours of the timetable to it thereafter, than schoolchildren in Britain devote to foreign languages. This island population, with its history of empire, has always rather felt that other countries should be learning its language and not vice-versa. America has continued this theme. How dominant would the English language now be if Columbus had colonised North as well as South America? Being an island may also have been a factor. It is possible that we have not been genetically programmed to pick up many languages, as have those groups who for centuries lived at the great crossroads of Europe and with many neighbours.

Entry into the European Community was supposed to change all this, and perhaps may do so in the future. These things take time. But we are still receiving many children into the ML classroom who do not see the point of learning the new subject and have to be motivated by the teacher. We are thus in a different position from the teacher of Maths, Science and English, and must provide, where there is little intrinsic motivation, extrinsic incentive to learn.

I firmly believe that the key to successful language teaching is the enthusiasm of the ML teacher her/himself. However, when I started teaching I found that love of my subject and the desire to communicate that love to my pupils was not enough. Nor was humour, light-heartedness, knowledge of the learning process, respect for the difficulties of that process or affection for young people. Indeed, some of these could be counter-productive. My work was stressful because I was having to try too hard in terms of time and energy to get things across to my classes, who were not sufficiently interested. I began to have feelings of failure. It was stressful for them too. We were engaged in a rather dismal dance, in which I tried to make them do what they didn't want to do, and they resisted. They became either bored or resentful. In short, they did not want to learn what I was offering.

What I really needed, and did not have, were *practical* techniques for expressing my enthusiasm and engaging theirs. Which activities would make the foreign language interesting, enjoyable and relevant, and which would not? What would suit my particular style of teaching, and also the particular style of learning of each class? I wanted to give children a sense of mastery, and control over their own learning – how was that to be brought about? How were learners of every conceivable range of ability to be kept working together at their own pace, without being bored, and at the same time stretching the high-flyers? Which is more valuable – enthusiasm or ability? What ways could I find to interest individuals in independent learning? Can they be forced to do homework? In what ways can slow or reluctant workers be motivated to go on, and to improve?

What about co-operative effort, and using the various talents of pupils to benefit the class as a whole? Could the strong be induced to help the weaker students? Could those who struggled achieve the same satisfaction as the high-achievers? And what about competition – can there be competition without demoralisation? Is it possible to pay equal attention to everyone in the class, including the 'quiet ones' (who sometimes believe that the teacher does not speak to them very often because he/she does not like them!). Was I any good at relating to parents, and did it matter? In what ways was I going to bring the foreign country into the classroom and vice versa? How could I achieve my aims for learning whilst at the same time making my classroom a safe place where 'failure' was allowed, as a normal step along the road to success, and learners would feel secure because they were being valued for what they were and not for what they knew? And most of all, how could I fill my classes with enthusiasm and maintain that enthusiasm over the years?

Over many years, I learnt that successful language learning only takes place when tasks are brought within the scope of the learner, and when rewards and achievement are built into every activity. But it is far from obvious how this is to be done. Below are some of the practical techniques I have used with children of all ages and abilities. When parents come into school on parents' evening and ask how it is that their child actually *likes* French, and 'can do it too', as they themselves never could, you know that you must be doing something right. I hope these ideas will prove as useful to you as they have to me.

Note

1. Footitt, H. (2000) Losing our tongues just when we need them. *Guardian Higher Education*, 1st February 2000, 3H.

Chapter 1
Keeping sane

Q Becoming a teacher of modern languages – why do we do it?
Q ML teaching – easy option or nightmare?
Q How to cope with the four skills
Q Where do feelings of failure come from?
Q What is the secret of success?
A It is the only available career which really appeals to you, and you have no idea what will be involved
A Far more difficult than you expected, but also far more rewarding
A Break down your tasks into simple units with which you can feel secure
A Trying to do too much too soon
A Retaining the enthusiasm of your learners

In at the deep end!

Welcome to the modern language teaching profession! For some years now you have enjoyed travelling to the sunnier climes of Europe, and imbibing the fruit of the vine (there is no avoiding it!) You have admired the style and verve of the unEnglish, and cannot deny that you have picked up a little of their eloquence and elegance yourself. As a result you have come to feel that your true vocation may lie in this area. But you have a problem. At last the hour you have long dreaded has arrived – graduation. Your student loan has reached unheard of proportions and neither the state nor Daddy will support you in your chosen way of life a moment longer. Decision time has arrived   you must leave the groves of academe and find a job.

Air stewardess or translator?

You have dismissed the idea of becoming an air stewardess or steward (how old is too old?), or a tour representative (adore package tours?). You would really love to do translating or interpreting (bilingual or a genius?) and highly paid secretarial work is tempting (speak two foreign languages and like offices?). Somehow you are not quite suited to any of these. So what remains? Well, as your mother used to say, 'there is always teaching'. Suddenly, you look at teaching in a different way and it begins to assume a rosy glow. Yes, you had left school vowing never to go back, but wait a minute, what about those long holidays and early afternoon departures? The teacher friend you have in France who spends every afternoon on his surf board? Permanent contact with the foreign country you love, and all those free school trips? The respectful hush in the classroom and those eager faces looking up at you, yearning to be filled with knowledge? And, best of all, sitting on the other side of the desk at parents' evenings – revenge at last? You quite like children, they quite like you, so why not teach them French, Spanish, Italian or German? What could be easier? After all, this is a profession where you start with many years experience at the receiving end, so it's obvious that you know how it's done. In no time at all you will have the whole class rattling away like native speakers!

First encounter with the National Curriculum

When you arrive at your first school, however, you find it is not quite as you imagined. You find that you are not, after all, going to do your own thing. A considerable shock awaits you. You are introduced to that great national monument: 'The National Curriculum'! This document strikes fear into the heart of the boldest of readers. There are also frightening things called SATS, regular national tests to reveal exactly what your class has (or has not!) learnt, and something else you had forgotten all about – classes of bored children! Even, yes, children who do not like French, Spanish, Italian or German and have no desire whatsoever to learn them. It is hard to imagine, and it is not what you had expected. At first sight, you are discouraged by the enormity of the task before you. But do not fear, this is a normal reaction. What could be more natural? Teaching languages is not an easy option, and you are beginning to find that out. Language learning is divided into four areas, and the skills required for each are all quite different. Not only do they vary greatly in difficulty but each one requires completely different teaching methods.

Keep calm

Do not be afraid, all is not lost. The good old National Curriculum, scourge of teachers who were in schools during the early nineties, need no longer fill you with dismay and feelings of inadequacy. Its complexity was beyond human comprehension, and I am proud to say that I lived through the introduction of the original document, which divided up language teaching into myriad tasks of unbelievable complexity, all written down in excruciating detail using almost incomprehensible prose. Thanks to the teacher troops who went over the top before you, and their vociferous protests, the new and modified NC slipped quietly in with the new millennium, and is a considerably simplified document. Don't worry about it. Just find out from your co-ordinator how it is interpreted in your school (because all is in the interpretation), and get on with it.

Taking the bull by the horns

Ignore the National C. for the moment, but don't forget to keep your eye on the ball. What is the ball in language teaching, you might well ask? The ball, I'm afraid, is examination success. That is what you will be judged on, what your school will be judged on and what you will have to have in mind from the earliest years. The four skills to be examined will be listening, speaking, reading and writing. In real life, all the skills are learned together in an interconnected jumble, but in the classroom, you have to be aware of each separately. It's simpler therefore to divide your teaching task into these four areas from the beginning. Ask yourself exactly what has to be learned in order to be proficient in each of the four areas:

(1) *Listening and responding* = lots of practice in listening to tape recordings of authentic French and answering questions about them. Main problem: finding sufficiently easy material at the right speed for the first year or two.
(2) *Speaking* = memorising and repeating fluently some common conversations. Main problem: motivation.
(3) *Reading and responding* = learning a wide range of new words (including different parts of the verb). Main problem: avoiding boredom.
(4) *Writing* = memorising and writing, with correct spelling if possible, some simple material e.g. a short letter. Main problem: many children cannot achieve this in their own language, let alone a foreign one …

You are not Hercules

I have enjoyed working with foreign language teachers both here and abroad and I have found them on the whole to be, like me, a conscientious lot. I suppose learning to speak a second language involves a touch of perfectionism in the first place. To be done successfully it must be done correctly, and with a good eye for detail. Chemistry teachers do not expect every pupil to become a chemist, but second language teachers really do want every pupil to speak good German, Spanish or whatever. This expectation sometimes creates extra tension in the learning process, raised teacher blood pressure, and debilitating feelings of failure. These feelings of failure stem from:

The three common delusions of the beginning ML teacher:

(1) Children want to learn the language you want to teach them.
(2) Learning a foreign language is easy.
(3) All you need is a good coursebook.

A learner teacher in a no-win situation

I began teaching with no teacher training whatsoever and therefore underwent a long period of probation. Part of the probation procedure involved the headmaster standing outside my door and listening to what was going on inside! A somewhat riotous atmosphere had developed, as tended to happen, inexplicably, to my lessons in those days. My headmaster was a gentle and kind man, and naturally concerned. He enquired in a well-meaning sort of way, what exactly I had been doing at the time of his inspection. I explained to him innocently that I had been writing out on the blackboard the difference between the Perfect and the Imperfect tense, with examples and questions, the whole of which they were supposed to be copying into their exercise books. I could not understand his raised eyebrows. This was a Year 10 class, what could be more useful, essential even, for them to learn? The fact that they were not listening, learning (or doing) anything at all, had escaped my idealistic notice. I was too busy imparting knowledge. Aside from issues of class control (!), this was the moment of my first, and most important realisation – you can only teach learners what they want to learn.

You can reduce your stress levels

If you are working with mixed ability classes, accept from the start the fact that you are not going to be able to teach all the things on our skills list to *all* the children. Divide the learning load up into what you can realistically hope to achieve, and do not try to teach everything to everyone. Some will never learn to spell in French, some will never write well or at all. You are not to blame. This is not to do with good or bad teaching, it is to do with the innate ability of the child in those particular areas. Always bear in mind that a child is unlikely to be able to do in French what he cannot do in his native language. The different levels of exam paper allow for these ability gaps, and setting will hopefully transform the situation in Years 10 and 11. So do not worry too much about writing for the first two years, and concentrate on what the class *can* do. Do not discourage yourself and do not discourage the children.

Beware of 'old fogies'

The staffroom is a very important place for you, especially when you are new and lack confidence. This is the place where you will forge your identity, and where you must acquire most of your information and feedback. Assemblies and department meetings are not enough. Listen and you will find out how the school works. Most of your colleagues will be supportive, especially those in your own department. But never assume everyone will be on your side. As in any other group, each staffroom has it's quota of individuals with personality problems. If snide comments are made, ignore them, and don't take it personally. Within a day or two you will have picked up which are the colleagues you can learn from and work with, and which are not. You will also quickly identify who are the 'old fogies'. These are the people who have been at the school since time immemorial. They can be of use on matters of information such as where were surplus tape recorders stored before the inspection of '89, or how do you get keys for the store cupboards in your room, but ignore any comments they have to make on teaching methods. Their teaching methods will be as prehistoric as their careers. If one of them should start to mutter in the staffroom about yours, just remind yourself, silently of course, of their doleful French classes, and remember the lack of enthusiasm or achievement they engender by their noble pursuit of 'high standards'.

Simplification is everything

Around you in the staffroom you will notice teachers with a wild-eyed look. Say nothing – it is from too much reading of the National Curriculum. Take care not to become one of them. Just think of it like this – the class has four or more years to acquire the following, in order of difficulty:

(1)   a large store of new words;
(2)   recognition of new words by hearing only;
(3)   fluency in common conversations;
(4)   spelling of new words;
(5)   ability to write from memory some simple material.

Let's narrow this down even further. For the first two years you can safely ignore the last two requirements. So you have only three main areas to address from the beginning. This is reassuring. Of course, there still remains the problem of the sheer volume of material to be covered, but that is not where your real difficulty lies. As a new teacher, your most challenging task is not the passing on of knowledge. If this is the only thing you have in mind, and if you dedicate your teaching time to it, you will be disappointed far more than you are satisfied, and your lessons will be dispirited affairs. You will find that learning is not taking place as you had hoped, in fact some children will be wasting their time. Only the bright few will be achieving anything.

You are on your own

What you have to do is to harness your own enthusiasm into finding ways in which to engage, and retain, the initial enthusiasm of the beginner. And there is only one way of doing so – by providing success and enjoyment in all your learning activities. And only you can do this. I have suffered from a common delusion throughout my teaching life. It is to do with coursebooks. It is particularly strong whenever a new course is introduced by one of the language publishers. The delusion consists of a belief that the new course will provide *everything* that my classes need for successful learning. Looking at the expensive, brightly coloured new coursebook, full of cartoons and quizzes and puzzles, you may know the feeling: how can I fail? Many of the latest courses use humour to good effect and have a splendid variety of materials and activities, attractive layout and beautifully coloured illustrations. (Visit the Centre for Information on Language Teaching in Covent Garden[1] *before you buy anything* – you can see it all there). They have an air of gaiety and promise about them too, which is vital. But they are not enough. All is in how the teacher uses them. You will find this from the very first page. The most entertaining coursebook can be as dull as ditchwater with a dull teacher, and they cannot inspire a class which does not want to learn. Only you can do that. A course like this can be an important, even an essential, aid but in the end, you can rely on no-one but yourself to create the atmosphere of excitement and interest which will keep your classes learning over the long term. Before we go on to think about teaching methods which will achieve this, let's think about what I consider to be one of the main causes of lack of enjoyment in modern language learning – anxiety.

Note to Chapter 1

1. The Centre for Information on Language Teaching and Research, 20 Bedfordbury, Covent Garden, London WC2N 4LB. Tel. 020 7379 5082.

The National Curriculum is unveiled, 1992

Chapter 2

Creating confidence

Q Does speaking in a foreign language come easily?

Q If fear of failure is normal, how can we get rid of it?

Q What does an anxiety-free first lesson for any age group look like?

Q Is homework fun?

Q Is homework assessment always possible?

Q Apart from thumbscrews, what techniques can be used to extract work from homework defaulters?

A Most of us find speaking to an audience intimidating, even in our own language

A By making sure the task is within their grasp

A Give them a very short speech act, attractively presented, and lots of practice

A I have not yet found a way to make homework fun. Other things are always more fun. Please write to me if you have!

A It has to be as constant and inescapable as the sword of doom. It is the only way to actually get homework done by *all*

A After one chance to catch up at home, it must be done at school *in their own time*

Anxiety – the demon of foreign language learning

Even confident adults find speaking in front of others difficult. Ask any best man. To speak in a new and strange language is even more intimidating. Children dread it. This is a perfectly natural reaction and one of the main reasons learners 'don't like French!'. It is your first and most important task to reduce this anxiety, and there are many ways in which it can be done. Firstly, have a friendly chat with the class before any teaching and share their anxiety. Make it clear that what they are feeling is normal. Then point out that we are all born with an innate speaking ability which varies from person to person and is not under our control. It can be developed, obviously, but with wide differences in effort needed. Some will find it easier to learn to speak a foreign language than others, just as some are born better performers at athletics or music. They will easily accept this idea, and be relieved. Perfection is not expected after all! Tell them that some will learn a lot, some less. Speaking ability is not a matter of intelligence. Make sure they understand that the speaking ability we already have when we approach a new language is to do with how well we speak in our own, which in turn depends on how much we have spoken, and been spoken to, in our lives so far. To achieve a good standard, all we have to do is practice. Remove the idea of failure. Fear of failure is the main reason learners hold back from speaking in a new language.

Achieving high standards?

You may fear that if you do not insist on 'high standards' (e.g. perfect pronunciation and intonation) none will be achieved. Don't worry. You will find that 'standards' have a way of looking after themselves. Does this sound ludicrously optimistic? I'm afraid it may, yet the fact is that I noticed quite early in my teaching career that children have a built in desire to *get things right*. They always know when they are not getting it right and do not need to be told. Criticism will not lead to improvement, nor will it motivate them, quite the opposite. They are their own best critics, and will strive for good results, provided that the task is within their grasp. In my opinion, the second most important skill you can bring to teaching (I have mentioned the first in Chapter 1), is the ability to construct tasks which are achievable by the learner, whatever their level of competence. Not only must they be achievable, they must be immediately seen by the learner to be so. In this way, initial anxiety is relieved and the task will be approached with enthusiasm. You will have noticed how coursebooks with an explanatory and instructional style which is above the level of some of the readers (especially if it is in the target language) can inhibit them to the extent that they are convinced from the start that they 'can't do it' and therefore cannot. Confidence may not always be restored by teacher intervention. To begin with, a small card with an even smaller amount of writing on it provides a very safe and easy-to-achieve task which will boost confidence and enable them to attack the work with enthusiasm. Remember also that they will help each other to achieve, if the climate is right. You can create that climate.

Creating the right climate

After your talk, address their anxiety by going straight into a first speaking task. It must be pairwork, so that they can support one another, easily achievable at their level, and not more than two lines each. A simple 'hello' conversation suited to their age, written by them on card which they will keep as part of a collection. Why on card, you may be asking? Isn't that rather a lot of trouble and expense to be going to? Definitely not. Children *love* cards (as any parent in the grip of the Pokemon craze will tell you). I say 'children', but there is no age limit to their appeal. Young ones like to handle them, decorate them, show them, hoard them; older ones like their permanence, the way they can be individualised and organised, perhaps using IT. As their collection increases they will come to value it in a way they do not value what they write in an exercise book. Not only will they be able to take the cards home to work on, they will have visible proof of what they have learnt. Year 5 learners will be proud to show their family what they can do. Most will be challenged to make their cards attractive. (Who wants to have a box full of scruffy cards?)

Why bother?

Of course, all these things can also be done with an exercise book, but only in theory. Children do not care about exercise books in the way they care about cards. This is another of those inexplicable facts of life we just have to accept. Try and have brightly coloured card, which the younger children will enjoy decorating and making attractive (and not only the younger ones either). And remember that these cards will be around long after old exercise books have hit the bin. Making and decorating them can be a form of relaxation, one of the frequent 'rest breaks' which can relieve the tension, and contribute to the enjoyment, of your lessons. Make it your practice, whenever you sense a feeling of staleness or lack of interest in the room, to change to another activity. This is very important, as a means of maintaining interest and motivation *for all*. If even one member of the group is not involved, regard yourself as failing, and move on.

The perils of homework

Before they begin to copy the card, begin working on it in ways outlined in Chapter 14: 'Speaking', and when both card and pronunciation are ready, ask them to take them home to practice. Suggest they enlist the help of family members if possible. The family will probably be interested in the early stages, and their involvement can be a great help to the learner, even if their knowledge of the particular language is nil. What fun to teach your mother a few words of Italian or French! Next lesson, begin assessing what they have achieved. Let them practice the conversation in pairs whilst you go round the room giving them a mark between 5 and 10, no lower. Do not start marking until a pair has volunteered that they are ready. It is never a good idea to start reviewing homework from cold, as many who actually did make an effort to learn their card, will have forgotten with the passage of time, and need a moment to remind themselves of it. Like gymnastics, the brain needs a warm-up. One day's exposure to new material is *never* enough. This method of checking homework avoids anxiety – you are not performing 'in public', and creates a sense of achievement – you do get a reasonable mark which takes into account effort as well as achievement. If you feel that there has been no effort to be rewarded, treat the pair as homework defaulters. But beware, there is one thing you have to watch with this otherwise admirable system of marking – your attention. Because you are attending to individual pairs, the system can only work if every child is involved in an activity of some sort. Those who finish first must always have something to do – ideas later (Chapter 8: 'Working independently').

What to do when the budgie dies or granddad eats the card

The reasons children conjure up for not doing homework are wild and wonderful to hear, and can brighten your whole day. They are a constant source of amusement in the staffroom and recounting them is an easy way of gaining prestige. The two I mention above are almost pedestrian, as they were invented by me and my adult imagination, but they reflect the general flavour. There will always be one or more of your class who have not done their homework. It is another of those unaccountable facts of teaching life. Or could it just be human nature? Do not feel responsible in any way. Learn to live with it. Teachers have been known to lose their tempers entirely with particular offenders, resorting to an ever-escalating scale of punishments. They find themselves supervising double-treble-quadruple detentions (no-one else will!) and the whole thing becomes a personal struggle. That way madness lies. Your function is not to punish or to berate, but to *get it done*. Every piece of learning not done is a step on the road to failure. If they claim something has befallen the original (and this is a strong favourite), give them a new blank card and decree that it must be completed and learnt for the next lesson. They will of course have no mark to be entered in their record book – which does not please their sense of symmetry. If they do not comply then you must bring on the big guns – valuable break time (theirs, not yours) given up to do the learning. Let them stand outside the staffroom or wherever suits you, but don't feel obliged to supervise them. You will be surprised how rapidly learning can take place when friends are waiting in the play-ground. This strategy should be embarked on more in sorrow than in anger on your part. Describe it as their own choice, not yours, and arrange for classmate help if they are having problems. Never allow undone homework to take up *your* time.

Time is too valuable to do homework

If you intend it to be done, every piece of homework must be marked. Learners have a natural disposition to regard homework as some sort of inconsequential add-on extra. They have no natural incentive to complete it. I think the reasoning goes something like this: it is not done at school, therefore it is of no importance. It can only be a personal whim of the teacher, or revenge for the suffering they endured in their own schooldays. Speaking homework is an even more outrageous imposition. Every child knows in its bones that 'speaking' cannot be a task in itself, and is of no importance in any other subject. Therefore it is down to you to provide the incentive to strive, and an excellent way to supply this is by assessment: unavoidable and relentless assessment.

Where on earth is the time to come from?

The logistics of listening to 30 individuals speak whilst at the same time main-taining supervision of the group are formidable. It is a time-consuming business. How can you devote great chunks of your time to listening to pairwork without taking your eyes off the rest of the class? There are several ways to approach this. Having children out to your desk whilst the class gets on with something else is an obvious way and has the advantage that you can see the whole group more easily. But it is a great embarrassment to less-than-perfect performers. No-one is ever so involved in their work that they do not listen to other peoples' oral efforts, with titters where appropriate. Communal listening, perhaps, with the class sharing the assessment, is an alternative which can be fun and productive, but only with a confident, high-ability group. Taking individuals into the corridor leaves the class unsupervised and probably rioting. Recording all on tape and taking it home to mark leaves no room for that vital instant feedback (and has been known to lead to divorce). Mixed-ability children respond to immediate feedback and cannot cope with long gaps between performance and evaluation. So try to work in the room, progressing round the class, but always taking up a position where you can see everyone (move the pair if necessary) and above all, working at *speed*.

Speaking test as Olympic sprint

Speed can be achieved in the following ways:

(1) Listen to pairs in order of volunteering. In this way you do not waste time listening to the halting efforts of those who are not ready. It also gives less able pairs more time to prepare. Do not argue with any pair who claim to be 'not ready' by the end of your tour. Keep them behind at the end of the lesson and treat as homework defaulters (see above).

(2) Do not correct mistakes or draw attention to them. (A nightmare for the typical linguist, but you will get used to it!) If you feel the pair have noticed where they went wrong and are anxious about it, do not halt the flow, but wait until you can quickly repeat the correct words at the end of the conversation.

(3) Do not allow eager beavers to 'have another go'. I know this is very, very hard for caring professionals to do. But you must resist the waving hands, the urgent pleas, the jumping up and down, the wailing. This part of your lesson must not drag on or it will not work. Pretend you are taking part in an Olympic sprint. As you speed up, so will the other participants.

(4) Give feedback to each pair, but very briefly. In a couple of words praise what they have achieved or the effort they have made.

(5) Mark from 5 to 10 only. If you feel no effort has been made, treat as homework defaulters (at the end of the lesson). Do not make a big production out of it. Be cheerful. Some pupils enjoy negative attention as much as praise. Some enjoy it more!

Marks to enjoy

Recording their marks as you progress round the room will delay you significantly. It may seem to be the work of a moment, but during that moment your attention will be taken away from the class and what is going on in the room. When this happens repeatedly, after each conversation, you are sending out signals to the rest of the group to remove *their* attention from the lesson also. (You will have noticed what happens when a colleague comes in to talk to you when you are teaching).

There is no real necessity to do so in the early stages, and no time either. However, if they are keen, you could let them record their own marks, as a good way of reinforcing feedback, of adding continuity to the learning process, and of emphasising the importance of speaking work. And most of all, because they love it!

Learn to love the system

This system of marking speaking homework avoids anxiety and creates achievement in several ways. Firstly, although the work was intended to be done at home, time for revision in class has allowed a second chance to reach a good standard. Purists may moan that high-flyers might be able to do all the learning required in the classroom, thus avoiding homework altogether. This is quite true, but does it actually matter? It can be done at home, on the bus, in the bath, at a football match as far as I am concerned, as long as it is done! Secondly, the fact that a mark is going to be awarded in a few minutes time seems to galvanise a class into action somehow, and increase the incentive to do well. I am not sure why this is. Could it be that the powerful procrastination instinct has been switched off? Thirdly, working together with a partner means that each can help the other to improve by pooling their common knowledge. The stronger can coach the weaker, in order to achieve a satisfactory mark. Lastly, and perhaps most importantly, with the exception of the final couples, there is less chance of embarrassment caused by the rest of the class hearing your efforts. They are all busy practising themselves. They are not speaking alone.

No sooner learned than forgotten

Even a short learning task of this sort will quickly fade from view unless kept fresh by frequent use. All the cards must be reviewed regularly. As a new teacher I was profoundly shocked to find that work I thought had been thoroughly learned in one week seemed to have become a mere figment of my imagination by the next. Pupils seemed to find it an amusing eccentricity of mine to expect them to have remembered anything. I learnt a lot about 'revisiting'. So ask the class to bring suitable containers to keep the cards together, and have them handy in the classroom. Any card which is lost or defaced must be replaced. Use them at least once a week for a little role-play practice at the end of the lesson. This is usually a popular activity, giving the opportunity to be more active (Chapter 14). And do not underestimate the lively and imaginative ideas the learners will bring to their acting. They are your best resource. Meanwhile, be happy to have completed their first piece of language learning in a way which they found satisfying, enjoyable and, hopefully, as anxiety-free as possible.

Chapter 3

Your best friend – the Overhead Projector

Q Can you trust the blackboard?

Q How far should you go in order to get your hands on an OHP?

Q Why do they make learning more fun?

Q Do classes attend more to the OHP than to the blackboard?

Q Can you use children's skills without favouritism?

A No, because your precious notes may disappear, and in any case have to be tediously re-written too often

A Very far indeed!

A By removing the anxiety of not-knowing

A Yes, it seems screens have a fatal attraction in these televisual times

A Yes, by avoiding 'task as reward' (favouring the eager-to-please), and also 'task in turn' (which creates anxiety for a few)

Your eager audience

Before we go any further, let's consider one of the most important, and not often mentioned ways in which, with very little preparation, you can reduce stress for yourself and stress for your pupils in the classroom. You have planned your first lesson. You are eager to get started. If this is the class's first French lesson, they too are eager to get started. If this is *not* their first French lesson, then they may be slightly less eager to get started, or even (perish the thought) not eager at all. Perhaps they have already had a few years of failing to learn as much as they would have liked. If this is the case, you may be planning to stand at the front with a piece of chalk, and write things on the board. You have carefully planned the items you are going to write. You have planned them to be jewels of crystal clarity, which by the end of the lesson will have passed over into the children's minds. But take my advice – you are wasting your time …

The mysterious blackboard

What I am about to say may shock you. Unfortunately it applies to all boards, whether black, white or any other colour. (I shall include them all in the term 'blackboard' as they are all the same family with the same genes – not one is spared.) This genetic defect is of major importance to the teacher, and particularly to the teacher of modern languages, but is usually only appreciated years after the start of the teaching career. I feel it is my duty therefore to bring it to the notice of beginning teachers before it is too late.

If you teach subjects other than modern languages, and you probably do, you may already have noticed the mysterious, almost mystic properties of the blackboard. There is no consensus about this, but in my opinion, and in the opinion of some teachers (and many thousands of children throughout the land), the magic of the blackboard casts a spell. This spell works in three ways:

(1) Nothing written on the blackboard shall be understood.
(2) Nothing written on the blackboard shall be remembered.
(3) Nothing written on the blackboard shall be there for the next lesson.

The disappearing notes

There are few circumstances in which it is wise to *write up notes on the blackboard*. If you are lucky enough to have a room of your own, and laboriously prepare your board ready for the next lesson, you will find that should you for any reason leave the room, be it only for one second, an amazing variety of people will pass through, expunging your notes nonchalantly as they go. It is pointless to conduct an enquiry: even if you can track down the person involved (classes can be helpful with this), they will not always be able to give you a reason. It may spring from some deep atavistic teacherly instinct which cannot be controlled, it may be the work of a friendly cleaner or of a helpful child, but there it is …

The pupils' delight

On the other hand, do not think that you can win by writing up your material at the start of the lesson. Writing on the blackboard is a no-win situation. Whether you rush around the school from room to room or remain in one place, hurrying to write on the board before the class arrives means stress and hassle for you, and a slightly less than legible scrawl for the class. Do not be afraid to make a strategy decision and *just give up*. Do not think even for one moment of the one remaining alternative left to you – what can only be described as 'the pupils' delight' – their appreciation of the teacherly back view, turned to inscribe *during* the lesson!

Go into the head's study and weep

Avoid the blackboard like the plague. Get yourself an overhead projector! Every school has a few, lurking in cupboards, left over from one of the many fleeting crazes of teaching technology. You will be astonished by what you can find in these cupboards. Track them down. Talk to old timers on the staff, people who have been there since prehistoric times. They are an invaluable source of information, and the only people in the school who have the faintest chance of knowing where anything is. However, they will *not* know where the keys are. The keys are always lost. Do not be discouraged. The caretaker, your most useful colleague, is your man here – he will have ways of getting into these mausoleums. Like Parsifal after the Holy Grail, track your OHP down. Don't be afraid to be ruthless. Of course you will be considered eccentric, even deranged, but be strong. Bully whoever you have to bully. Beg your head of department. Bribe the head of resources. Make friends with parent governors. Go into the head's study and weep. But get your hands on an OHP.

Do not succumb to temptation

Congratulations: you are about to solve a major communication problem. But firstly, firmly decline all offers of a screen if you value your sanity. Secondly, pin an old sheet over the blackboard. Now your 'wonderful jewels' will live forever! But do not succumb to the 'luxury' of having a screen. This is taking technology too far. You may be in a state of euphoria at this stage, carried away by the technological marvel of it all. You have succeeded against all the odds, in actually acquiring the equipment you wanted – an unusual experience in itself – entirely by your own efforts. You are a source of wonder and envy to other staff. You may think a screen an offer you cannot refuse. Refuse it. The presence of a screen in the room presents all the problems of a blackboard but with far more possibilities for damage and interference. It is another war zone.

Your treasure chest – transparencies

How to describe the pleasure of not having to write on the white or blackboard any more? No more smelly whiteboard marker pens which make you sneeze, and constantly run out. No more searching for chalk, no more mess, no more dust up the nose, no more lost board rubbers, no more disgusting cloths, no more hidden board rubbers or chalk, no more theft by the teacher next door (yes!), no more struggling to write legibly in a hurry, no more interruptions from children sent by the teacher next door to borrow chalk, and no more moral agonising over whether or not to lend it … I could go on. Instead, beautifully set out and inscribed in your best writing in the calm planning atmosphere of home, extremely clear, with lots of white space between, and in as many colours as you like, the material you are trying to convey can be seen day after day, as long as it is needed, and taken away to be brought out next day or year, with other classes or whenever you like. It need never be repeated – think of that – whether a list of vocabulary, a simple conversation or something more complex. (I must mention that in my opinion it is never wise to use the word 'vocabulary' in front of the class – such a heavy word, fraught with pain and incomprehensibility. If you can bear it, call them simply 'new words', so much more friendly and biddable. Classes know that learning 'new words' might just be a possibility, learning 'vocabulary' much less likely …)

Let there be light!

Now you have achieved one of your major aims – to remove anxiety. The main teaching points are displayed for the class – in colour – on the OHP and your class can relax in the warm glow of having *Nothing to Remember*. They are free to direct all their attention to your fun-filled activities. What new material they need to know is all there on the OHP. But surely, you ask, that is making it too easy for them? How are they ever going to learn anything if it is all given to them without any effort on their part? But that is exactly the point. Strangely enough, precisely because the pressure has been removed, and they are handling the new material without anxiety, you will find that the majority will learn that material, some very quickly, some very slowly, one or two very little at all. (But the children who learn very little will have had fun.)

The secret of the OHP

The OHP allows your fun-filled activities to be more fun. If you are playing a familiarisation game with, say, numbers, the class will consult the OHP almost unconsciously, as if it were television. There are five advantages for the class:

(1) They do not have to take their eyes and their attention from what is going on in the game in order to find the information they require.
(2) They do not have to consult the new words they may have written in their exercise books.
(3) They do not have to flounder in the pages of your average textbook, far too crammed with material for a quick glance.
(4) Slow learners, who may also be slow readers, have a far better chance of finding out what they need to know from a screen in front of them containing only specific information. They simply do not have time to refer to the written word in their books.
(5) Referring to a book is anathema to many children, even those well able to do so. But they seem to respond to the OHP in a spontaneous way, as positive as some adults are negative.

The children of technology

Technology is the lifeblood of today's children. Watching a screen, be it computer or television, is second nature to them – they cannot help it. Their eyes will return to the screen again and again, and remain on it for long periods. (Have you found yourself in the same position on training days?) You will never see them gaze at a textbook or exercise book in the same way. And the more frequently the brain registers what it sees, the more familiarisation and therefore unconscious learning is taking place.

Unsuspected skills

The children will amaze you by the speed with which they learn to set up the machine and place the transparencies for you. You will discover unsuspected skills in unsuspected people. Some will be eager to copy the transparencies for you in their best writing – which I am assuming will be better than yours. In my experience at least half the class have better hand-writing and artistic ability than I do. This can be a whole new area of achievement for those who do not shine in others. Responsibility can be some children's strong point, and they long to show it. If they are very determined to do a good job and ask to take the transparency home to work on, trust them. Loan them a used folder and send them off. Why do I recommend a *used* folder? To decrease stress if the work is not returned for some imponderable reason ('dog ate it', 'baby ate it', 'Mum washed it'). If you are teaching children who tend to be routinely careless with belongings – their own or the school's – be prepared to allow for low standards in this area. Otherwise you are setting them (and most of all yourself) up for failure and stress. Remember, the child from the home where no-one takes care of anything, is the child who most needs the opportunity to be responsible.

Handing out tasks

In order to increase the confidence and self-esteem of the whole group, and not just the individual, I prefer to hand out valued tasks (setting up the OHP, putting up flashcards etc.) neither as rewards, nor in turn. 'Tasks as reward' favour those who are eager to please and make it difficult for those who are not, and who have their reputation to think of, to take part. 'Tasks by turn' increase the anxiety of the shy or fearful ('when is it going to be my turn?' – 'will I be able to do it?') Unless special talent is required (in which case I do not hesitate to be firmly selective and explain why) I start with one of the eager-beavers to begin with (although obviously not always the same one). As the task becomes more familiar there will be more and more volunteers, until they have almost all had a turn. In this way, there is no pressure on those who are afraid to try for whatever reason. Most will be caught up in the general enthusiasm and have a go. For the remaining few, make them more than one offer, in a light-hearted way, but never put pressure on them or let them feel inadequate. Always respect their right not to expose themselves. They probably have very good reasons for it.

Chapter 4

Close encounters of the flashcard kind

Q Why flashcards?
Q How do I make them fun?
Q Are school credit points a waste of time?
Q Is illustration just a means of passing the time?
Q Can two lessons a week be enough?
Q What about differentiation?
Q How many repetitions will lead to retention?
A Because they are a multi-sensory resource, use all the four skills and are ideal for games
A By involving the class in making and judging them, by providing painless repetition, lots of communal 'puzzling', enjoyable 'tests', challenge for quick learners, a chance to shine for all, serious artwork, and a sense of mastery throughout
A They can be motivating, but be sure they are seen by the rest of the school as well-earned
A The brain learns more effectively when visual and auditory stimuli are combined
A Memorisation requires more than twice-weekly repetition
A Give independent choice at all stages
A Use the cards for brief regular revision, which is the only way to ensure permanent retention

A large store of new words

Children have a innate interest in and aptitude for the acquisition of new vocabulary. Their natural curiosity finds the fact that 'table' also means 'table' in French but is pronounced differently, fascinating. The differences, as well as the similarities between words in the two languages entertain them too. It is never too early to explain why we have these words in common and not in common, and a little simple history will amaze them. (Try explaining how France and England once had the same king, and watch them not believe you!) I am always astonished at how little is taught in schools about the history of our nearest neighbour, so closely interwoven with our own. And yet they know vast amounts about the Egyptians. Most of my classes have never heard of Joan of Ark or Napoleon, but they can tell you everything about a pyramid.

Fun with flashcards

When it comes to the acquisition of vocabulary, or as I prefer to call it, 'learning new words', attractive flashcards are, in my opinion, the best option, despite the expense, I'm afraid. Learning lists devoid of intrinsic interest kills endeavour – the key word must be fun and games. There is no doubt that flashcards are expensive, and are often seen as an optional extra. Nothing could be further from the truth. The brain learns best from visual as well as auditory stimulus, including especially colour. If your school hasn't been able to afford the cards to go with your course, rummage through the store cupboards and see if you can find discarded cards from discarded courses. The old 'Action' flashcards were attractive, and more comprehensive than some modern courses. But do not be tempted to use really old-fashioned cards – the children will not relate to them. Full colour is vital. Some recent courses have economised by using only two or three colours on their flashcards. The impact is not the same.

Flashcard famine

Try and have everything pictorial for as long as possible. For those words which are not covered by flashcards you can make your own. Cut out a suitable picture from a magazine brought in by the children and stick it on card. Or ask for volunteers to draw one for you. Explain that you can't draw, even if you can. Children with little interest in learning languages can really shine in the artwork department, changing their whole attitude towards the subject. So much fun can be had at the production stage – you might have a class vote on which of the drawings offered is the best, and will therefore be used for the final card (why is the funniest always 'le cheval'?) – or you can have other classes guess the artist. Inter-class rivalry can be fierce, with the following class demanding to be allowed to produce a far superior card, often with good results. Class competition gets all the children's adrenaline running and has even been known to result in *moans* when the lesson is cancelled!

The guessing game

Use Blutack to stick six or so of the new flashcards on the board and write the French underneath. Ask the class if anyone knows what any word means. Of course, they always do. The obvious ones will be done in a flash (no pun intended), but let them puzzle over the rest as long as possible, because all the time they are being attended to, the cards and the new words are seeping into consciousness. Children of all abilities like to have a guess, and all guesses must be treated with respect, with lots of laughter for the truly hilarious ones.

Is your flashcard really necessary?

Work with not more than eight flashcards, fewer for younger classes, and do not be tempted by the clever idea I stumbled upon – why not speed things up by leaving out the easy words? After all, do they really need a picture to teach them what 'une carotte' means? Obviously they do not, but I discovered that without them, interest in and enjoyment of the game diminished greatly, especially for the slower learners. Perhaps knowing some of the words to start with has a part to play in increasing confidence in the learning process. A foreign language is not completely foreign after all!

Wasting time playing games

Having made sure by questioning that everyone in the room knows what the cards represent in English (not just what it is, but how it functions – especially important if your school is multi-ethnic. A child fresh from the Indian sub-continent may have no idea what a washing machine is!). The next step is to have them repeat the French for each picture, in unison, after you. To avoid the excruciating boredom of this process, ask individuals at random for the English after each picture Be sure not to make repetition the only point of the activity. Repeating in any language is an intrinsically tedious occupation, but has a major part to play. So try to keep it to a minimum and incorporate it into another activity. Use short bursts at frequent intervals and they will hardly notice what they are doing. Be careful to continue pointing to each card before you speak. It is easy to forget, but this adds another process to the activity and should never be omitted until confidence has been achieved.

Let the able perform!

The eager beavers will want to read out the whole lot in English, which they find very satisfying. Some classes will also enjoy 'speed trials' at this stage, competing to see who can read them out faster. These prepare the ground for the same game when the French has been learnt. But long before the cards are well known to all, move on quickly to a 'test'. (This is not a test of what they know, but a learning game, greatly appreciated by the learners – 'Can we do a test now, Miss?') It is important not to rush the initial introduction to the cards. Teacher instinct sometimes makes us feel guilty about spending too much time on 'childish' games, but notice that, as well as enjoyment, the children are gaining a sense of mastery over their own learning. Their confidence will be carried over into the further stages of learning and is invaluable. This mastery is what is often so difficult to provide for foreign language learners.

The therapeutic test

I use the word 'test' very loosely. There is nothing children love more than a test in which they cannot fail, and my French 'tests' are therefore not tests in the conventional sense, because nobody who tries can fail. This is the procedure:

(1)   I name one of the cards in French.
(2)   They repeat after me in French.
(3)   They look at the French on the board.
(4)   They write the English for the card in their test book.

I choose six words only, in order to increase the chances of success, and always hear everyone's mark at the end, on a 'hands up' basis. (What is the point in getting full marks unless you can boast about it?) Even more satisfaction can be had if children keep a special book for test marks. Much pride will be taken in looking through the totals, and a school credit mark of some sort can be given for a certain number of 'six out of sixes'. The children know that they are learning these new words, although they are apparently making no effort. In fact they are learning more than they know, because by repeating each word after me they are working on their speaking skills, and by identifying the French word with its card, they are working on their listening skills.

Artwork for achievement

A new activity is appropriate now, and a change from class learning to individual artwork is usually welcome. First, the French and English for each flashcard is written in the back of their exercise books, followed by illustrations in the front, with French titles only. These give a valuable break in class suspense and will be enjoyed by classes of all ages. Take them seriously. Make sure you go round the class and mark them, otherwise they may be skimped. By moving round the room you can observe ongoing work and comment on it, thus ensuring high standards. You can also correct the French as you go. It is important that the titles are correct. For poor writers, have them done in pencil first. Should you have a very poor writer in the group, do them yourself. Obviously the number of pictures done can be varied according to the ability of the pupil. Leave it to them to decide, and to select which cards to draw. Be sure to spot poor pictures before it is too late for them to be done again. Do not accept poor work. Here is a golden opportunity for less academic children to acquire merit marks on a regular basis. This is not a detail. Children's attitude towards a subject can be greatly influenced by the availability, or not, of merit marks. Just remember that in order to avoid criticism from other members of staff ('How come Kulwinder gets credits in French and nothing else?'), and to protect the prestige of your subject, it is up to you to ensure that yours are well-earned.

Keep moving

It is a mistake to sit at the front and have work brought out for marking as it is finished. With mixed-ability classes this is never a good idea. The more you move amongst them the more effort they will make. This is something to do with the fact that your presence and interest gives them confidence. Besides knowing that you will spot mistakes or poor effort straight away, they also find it easier to ask questions or to consult. Some of these children are not self-motivated, and your attention is what motivates them. This is particularly so in the case of modern languages. I have noticed that colleagues who spend most of the lesson at their desk often achieve mediocre results.

Display work as learning

Early finishers who like the idea can begin a really superior copy of one flashcard for the classroom wall or corridor, varying the picture in a creative way if they wish. This should take all their spare class time for at least a week, perhaps at home also, so that nothing second-rate is displayed. Nothing is more unappetising than a classroom wall covered with masses of drab, careless posters, which do nothing for the prestige of the subject or of the children who dashed them off. With some elementary help, learners of all abilities can produce acceptable art work, provided they use (or borrow from you) felt tip pens! However, they need to see the standard required first. (Have a chosen few from the year before on view at the start.) For language purposes, a poster should be brightly coloured and leap to the eye. For this reason, it cannot afford to have too much detail (e.g. those notorious seething pictures of 'la gare', which confused rather than enlightened every classroom in the land in days gone by). It should be a thing of beauty and interest which attracts the eye, otherwise it can convey nothing.

Short and sweet

I hope that your lesson will now be over. If you are obliged to teach French lessons of more than 35 minutes, you have a problem. In the days of the local authority adviser, it was possible to enlist his/her support in convincing the head that foreign language lessons cannot be effective if the class has only two double lessons per week, for obvious reasons. This exposure may suit some subjects, such as Art and PE, and it is certainly convenient for the organisation of the timetable. But it is death to modern languages. A child's maximum learning span for new material is thought to be only half an hour. After that, the time has to be filled with subsidiary activities. Consider also the repetition factor, ideally daily, so vital for languages. How much repetition can there be if the group meets only twice a week? And therefore, how much retention?

More than two lessons a week

An ideal programme of learning for modern languages would be thirty minutes per day. Not many schools can afford this, given the many other demands of the National Curriculum. But do fight for more than two lessons per week. If you have some sort of 'adviser', get his/her help. If your Head declares the whole thing impossible, try to find someone teaching another subject who would also like single lessons, perhaps music or maths, and form an alliance. Talk sweetly to whoever does the timetable and persuade him/her how easy the change would be to arrange for the following year, and how good for the children. How much more they would enjoy their French and what a happy place the school would become … If nothing works, and you are under thirty-five, move to another school!

Flashcards as class participation

For your next lesson, have only the French on the board and let the class put up the cards, one by one, using volunteers. It is fun sometimes to allow one person do them all and have the class vote on whether they have succeeded in putting them up correctly. Play this game before they are too proficient – their mistakes create fun and satisfaction for all. If mistakes are not spotted, don't jump in too soon. Indicate that all is not well and give plenty of time for class perplexity. Finally allow 'looking in books' so that the class gets used to solving its own problems without teacher help (as they will later by using a dictionary). Of course when anyone spots a mistake, they have to get out of their seat, come up to the board and change the cards around themselves. This increases class suspense (and laughter, when another mistake is perpetrated). Another opportunity for fun here, but the stronger drive will be towards 'getting it right'. You will be surprised how even the shyest member of the group will come out of his/her shell to do this, and do not be surprised if someone with a sense of humour comes out just to enjoy the fun. This is a good way to relieve class tedium, and, never fear, the strongest drive in the end will be towards 'getting it right'.

The second 'therapeutic' test

Next lesson, when the flashcards are in place, and pointing, plus class repetition of the French, has refreshed their listening skills, continue to quiz without written testing, until the time comes to ask if they are ready for a 'test' *without* the writing on the board. They like this dramatic moment. They will probably rise to the challenge, even if some of them are not quite ready. The 'test' is the same as the last, but with the French erased from the board and only a number under each card. You give the French, they repeat, and write the number of the appropriate card as their answer. You will find your classes fully aware that this is an important step towards mastery and they have an inbuilt desire to reach it, whatever their ability.

Differentiation or common sense?

For the purpose of differentiation, looking at the list of words in their book, which is intended to be used as a sort of dictionary, must be permitted. Always provide an avenue for *finding out*. Some of the more anxious may never need to look in their book, but need to be relieved of the fear of 'not knowing' For some slower learners this will be a permanent arrangement, but for most it will be temporary only. They will be very proud to stop looking, the moment they are able – and they will make sure that you know it. Perhaps a single look will be exchanged between you, but you will have been watching out for it. Be careful also to watch out for the ones who never succeed in closing their books. Be aware of their effort and let them see that you consider it of equal importance. Children are very alive to differentiation and it is amusing to note that everyone in the room will know who is looking up the words and who is not. Before the test begins, quick learners, who have no intention of consulting their notes, will close books with an ostentatious flourish, even moving them to some inaccessible spot, perhaps on floor, or window sill, in order to make their point.

Make room for challenge

When working with mixed-ability classes, give no indication of who is expected to look up new words in their book during the test and who is not. If you suggest that there should be no looking up, you are creating stress. Give them the choice. Give it to all. Let them take the responsibility for their own outcomes, and respect that judgment. They always know what they can achieve and they will strive to do better – provided their confidence has not been eroded, or boredom set in. Start by asking if anyone is ready to do the test entirely without looking at their book. Of course you know very well that some are more than able to do so, but it is vital for the more intelligent to see the work as a challenge. If you simply tell them what to do, you take away that vital spark of challenge so important for high-flyers. They must make their own choice of level, and have a consequent sense of achievement. They will leap in to challenge you, volunteering their own feats of memory etc. in their eagerness to shine. Do not fail to give them this opportunity.

'We learnt those last week, Miss!'

Two or three lessons using flashcards on the board for games and tests should be enough for all but the most slow-learning group. After that, all that is needed for revision is to quickly show the cards at the beginning of the lesson and have the children call out the French, first in unison, then by volunteers. If they have forgotten, call it out yourself – this has to be a quickly completed activity. (For some reason which has always escaped me, learners love to hold the cards and show them themselves whilst the class calls out. A good way to involve the less involved.) This is probably all that will be needed to complete the new words required for one unit. However, never underestimate the learner's ability to *forget*. At regular intervals, past flashcards will have to be brought out for revision, unit by unit. There are many games which the children enjoy. One of the best is 'Hunt the flashcard'. About eight cards are given out, very fast but visible to all, to those who want one. The aim is for one person to assemble all the cards by asking (in French, of course, including 'please', thank you' and 'sorry') for the card he thinks the other has. If you have the flashcard you are obliged to give it. The person who thinks s/he can find them continues until s/he makes a mistake, when the cards pass to the other. Much suspense can be created during this game, for the whole class, who have policing duties, and not just for the players. Enjoyable games lead to memorisation and improve motivation. Of course they must be tailored for the age group, but all years will appreciate them, years nine to eleven becoming ever more cut-throat and sometimes devising their own. Games ensure that your lessons will never be dull. We have to accept the fact that, unfortunately for the modern language teacher, long-term retention will not occur of its own accord. It is up to you to arrange for it to happen. Remember the teacher's motto: No retention without intervention!

Chapter 5

Every child's birthright?

Q Can you have classroom competition without demoralisation?
Q Which is more important, ability or enthusiasm?
Q Can you avoid jealousy?
Q The teacher's markbook – what for?
A Competition as entertainment can be an important spur to learning
A Enthusiasm must take precedence if all are to keep working to achieve their own potential
A Give equal attention to all
A To help the learner to feel more in control of his own progress

The thorny question of competition

Mixed ability teaching has failed some of our slower learners. What is not so often noticed is that it has also failed the high-achievers. It has tended to overlook the psychological need of the high-flyers to be able to excel, and not only that, but to be seen by their peers to do so. The basic human urge to excel is not something that should be denigrated or ignored, it should be used as the powerful motivator it is. Only thus can you avoid boredom for the more intelligent. Find ways for them to shine, however basic the work. All children thrive on competition. Remove it, and you remove a powerful impetus for learning. Why else would you see children hoarding test marks and comparing with others? Why would 16-year-olds beg for more conversations to learn for homework, if not to compete with their peers? This is a far more powerful motivator than the approach of the exam.

Competition as entertainment

For many, the approach of the exam can be more dispiriting than energising. For all but the supremely confident, the potential for failure has a way of seeming greater than the potential for success. A well-motivated proportion of your learners will work hard in order to do well in exams, but another not insignificant proportion will not. They become discouraged, usually by fear. Competition works better, and, of course, is longer-term. It can start from the first lesson, and it can be fun. As a learner teacher I was taught to avoid competition in the classroom. It was thought to discourage and otherwise humiliate the slow learners. I am not sure in what way it was thought to disadvantage the quick learners – encouraging an inflated opinion of themselves, perhaps, or some such brazen quality not allowed in this country! With experience, however, I came to see it as a valuable tool, provided that attention was paid to certain key areas.

Volunteers only please

Competition should only take place amongst volunteers, and no-one should be asked to take part, feel expected to take part, or worst of all, be forced to take part. Each child should make their own choice. Never allow your lesson to become a place where a sensitive child is put under undue pressure, or exposed to unacceptable levels of stress. This happens only too often in the school environment. If you can avoid these pressures you will benefit not only your pupils, but the prestige of your subject. Anyone who has ever come last in the sack race will remember how unwilling competition can destroy interest in a subject.

Enthusiasm or ability?

Competition for all can only be provided by careful differentiation. Let everyone achieve at their own level of ability. For example, if small groups are setting out to record a listening test on the topic of clothes for the rest of the class, you might have one group volunteering to prepare a simple tape in French (perhaps six descriptions of clothes e.g. 'une robe rouge') to be answered in English, whilst another group prepares a tape of the same material in English to be answered in French. Another group will want to record ten items in French, and yet another insist on a more sophisticated creation involving size, colour or price. Allow high-flyers to concoct as challenging a tape as they like, and those who choose to answer it. It can then be passed on to another suitable class. If two groups offer to do the same thing, let them each produce a tape and have a class vote on the 'best'. But beware of having the better linguists recording the tapes all the time. This is always a temptation. You will of course have a better result, but learning is not about making good class tapes. It is about individuals making individual progress. Be careful to let all enthusiasts have a go, whatever their ability, and give them appropriate help when needed. Enthusiasm is always more important than ability – if you show that you favour the latter, you are cutting out two thirds of your class and depriving them of their chance to succeed.

How to avoid 'elitism'

Do not allow the creation of a small elite who do *everything*. If you find this is happening, switch to activities such as acting out role-plays, where groups can be mixed high and low ability, and marks awarded for acting as much as spoken French. Aim at groups of three or four, and you will find them working together, the stronger helping the weaker linguists to perform. It is in their interests to do so, because this work will be marked as stringently as any other. In this way you make the point that role-play, and all speaking tasks, are not just an entertaining activity, but perhaps the most important aspect of learning a language. Record the marks assiduously, and be sure to award a proportion for humour. Poor linguists can often shine in this area and thus have their chance to achieve. Also, it's more fun.

The non-competitor as second-class citizen

Divide your attention equally between competitors, successful and unsuccessful, and the rest of the class. Those who choose not to compete must receive as much teacher time and interest as those who do. Walk around the room as much as possible and be aware of where each child is and what they are doing. Make sure they know that you know. The school system makes some children feel they will only be esteemed according to their success at learning. Remember, there are always ways for the teacher to appreciate a member of the class, whatever their ability in the particular subject being taught. You will also find that the proficiency of the more talented linguists in a class can be enjoyed by the rest, much as a football crowd enjoys the skill of the star players. Jealousy will only occur if the teacher creates it. The purpose of competition should be class entertainment. Never encourage participants to take it seriously.

Montagu and Capulet: the fight to the death

Inter-class rivalry can bring a whole new dimension to the meaning of competition. If you are lucky enough to teach more than one class in the same year, of similar ability range, you will be able to experience competition of an intensity you never dreamed of! I once taught four Year 8 classes at once, and the prospect filled me with apprehension. How was I to maintain my interest and enthusiasm, how was I to cope with presenting the same material four times and still know where each class was? Sticking strictly to a lesson plan has never been my style. I prefer to let the lesson go where it needs to go (as far as possible within the confines of the curriculum!) and make up for 'lost' time later. I use the term 'lost' time in inverted commas, because it seems to me to be sometimes the most important time of all …

The best year's work I ever had

However, in this case, the only solution to the confusion problem seemed to be to keep all four strictly parallel and never allow one or other to get ahead. Although an emergency measure, and much against the grain, this turned out to be most fruitful. After one lesson the classes quickly picked up the fact that they were all doing exactly the same learning, and homework, and began to swop results, in the time-honoured fashion of learners everywhere. This informal interchange began to snowball. As time went on, their desire to outstrip each other knew no bounds. Every day they would leap (literally) into the classroom demanding to know what marks the last class had received for the last piece of work. If it was a homework conversation, for example, I would tell them first, without naming names, how many had achieved full marks and secondly, what the lowest mark had been. This was a matter of supreme interest to them. Piercing looks would go round the room, as they assessed how and by whom the other group's result was to be outclassed. They were determined to outstrip the other classes, all of them. Woe betide the good linguist who had failed to do his homework and produce the goods. Steps were taken to ensure that *nobody*, but nobody, scored zero. For some reason, a tradition arose whereby each of the classes left a rough record of the numbers achieving top and bottom marks on the board for the next class to see, and these were hotly contested. A close watch had to be kept to avoid sabotage (even though I had a full record in my markbook)!

Detailed records: a waste of teaching time?

It is very important for children to be able to see a record of their marks, good or bad. If you are totally aware of the standard of each child's work, keeping a detailed mark book seems at first to be a tedious waste of time. As a beginning teacher, I had the idea that the mark book was for my use only. I resolved to keep only a few chosen marks for the benefit of parents on parents' evening. I didn't need marks to tell me where individuals were with their work. But this was before I was taught by the children the real usefulness of a markbook.

Why will they give their right arm for a markbook?

It was obvious from the first that classes enjoyed keeping their own record of class-room test marks in the back of their exercise book, although I was not sure why. Interest knew no bounds when I took under my wing some small memo books, found abandoned, which they could use to record marks *only*. These small books became very important – why I did not know. Obviously, it must be gratifying for those with good results, but what about the rest? Wouldn't they prefer to forget all about theirs? I could see that this was not the case. But what were they getting out of it? And what is more, why did I find them peeping surreptitiously at my own markbook when at my table, and why were they so keen to examine the whole page, and everyone else's marks, minutely, for a very long time indeed, if given the chance?

The magic of the markbook

I can only surmise that what they see in their own personal markbook is a concrete pattern of their own progress, and what they see in mine is a concrete pattern of the progress of others with which to compare their own. I have noticed that, unlike the teacher, children do not seem to have the skill of assessing their own achievement in a general way, or the ability to feel confident that they are doing well (or not). They do not have the background information and ability to assess overall. So a list of marks means clarity and empowerment. Of course, the child with excellent marks has a whole range of satisfactions on viewing the markbook, feelings of achievement which s/he deserves. Comparison with others is chief among them. But what of the children with a list of poor marks, what does such an unpromising list mean to them?

To change or not to change?

They see a way to improve matters, to influence their fate. How? By getting a better mark next time! If even one of their marks is better than the rest, they have the satisfaction of improvement. They may resolve to aim at three instead of two next time. Or they may compete with a friend who has similar marks. It matters not if these two have the lowest marks in the class – competition will lead to improvement. Whether they succeed or not is not the issue – seeing their pattern of marks gives them a feeling of empowerment and control. They know where they are, for better or for worse. How reassuring this can be. It is surprising how little confidence most learners have in their own level of achievement. They depend almost entirely on the teacher's estimate. If test papers were to be mixed up, and a good mark issued to a poor student, or vice versa, there would be little protestation. It is as if learners are never quite sure how they are doing. But their marks building up slowly through the term, give them a clear and unmistakeable indication of what they are, or are not, achieving, along with a picture of the achievement of others. In this way, they are helped to take responsibility for their future progress, by deciding to change or not to change.

The markbook from hell

Another function of the detailed markbook shared with the class, is to advertise the importance the teacher attaches to their work. Slow learners in particular are sometimes awestruck on seeing for the first time their marks recorded in a large, official-looking book for all to see. It has not happened to them before. Suddenly they feel their work is important and that it is up to them to do something about it. They begin to care more. However, there may be one small problem with the public sharing of your classroom records. The pages of your markbook, like mine, may tend to be scruffy. Whether this is the result of a natural lack of neatness not remedied by years of teaching others to be tidy, or because everything has been jotted down swiftly in the heat of the moment (or both) is impossible to say. If you also occasionally find yourself, very briefly of course, in this position, do not despair. You will find many willing volunteers prepared to re-do the page in writing far better than yours. This is a task which need not go to the high achievers, but *must* go to a reliable and accurate pair. (Be sure to check after the first few lines – there can be no leeway here.) There is usually at least one special person in each class who has a talent for painstaking work and careful copying, who takes pride in what they produce and who has enormous patience. They will help you. They may not be high achievers, but they are people who will go far, and it is a privilege to teach them.

Chapter 6

A star is born

Q Is all the time and effort worthwhile?
Q Will they want to take part?
Q Where can I find suitable scripts?
Q What if it isn't 'all right on the night'?
Q Do I choose the cast for acting, or French-speaking, ability?
Q What if they can't manage the French?
Q If the audience can't understand it, won't they be bored?
Q How can I avoid drop-outs?
Q Can all vital events take place on stage?
Q Can drama be useful in other areas?
A Drama can improve foreign language acquisition, confidence, self-expression, co-operative skills, staff–pupil relationships, and the prestige of your department!
A They will if you start small to give them confidence, and let the project gain its own momentum
A You can't; write your own
A It won't be, and the audience will love it!
A For maximum commitment, the class should choose both cast and title
A Give them card aids, or reduce (or cut out) the French. If it's beyond them, do the next best thing
A Yes, so use techniques which will make the language accessible
A By making the play their own
A No, but it doesn't matter. Do the next best thing
A Yes, but beware of the staff concert!

'Je suis la plus belle!'

Children are natural actors. More fun can be had from acting out a simple French play than from any other language-learning activity yet devised by man. Teachers understand the satisfactions and gains in confidence children find in drama. The shy can enjoy expressing themselves in non-speaking parts. But for modern languages, there is an additional reward. The few words each child has to say make a deep and lasting impression, and if simple enough, will never be forgotten. The best lines become familiar, and you will hear them being repeated around the school, not only by the actors themselves either. I particularly remember a large Asian boy of thirteen, with poor English and even poorer French, who played a truly comical Ugly Sister in one of our French productions. He became famous for his performance. He looked so amazing that people quite unrelated to the cast brought in items for his costume. Years later, when he had left school altogether, we met in the street. Judge my astonishment when he came over to speak to me, and announced: 'Je suis la plus belle!' I'm pretty sure he knew what it meant, too!

Music, Maestro, please!

Of course, the children must not be aware of the true objective of the play. For them it must be fun. Everyone must be able to take part, some without speaking any French at all. The most important thing is to make it short, amusing, gory, with lots of colourful costumes, exciting action and, above all, *music*. Try and choose a story which lends itself to musical interlude or background. The most enjoyable moment is always the going-to-work song of the dwarfs in 'Snow White', or the waltz at the ball in 'Cinderella'. Using tape recorder and your local music library your opportunities are limitless. I found four different versions of the 'Marseillaise' to choose from for my French Revolution, and life and vigour was brought to the whole play by its frequent use.

Choose a universal story

Another important point to bear in mind is that, to succeed with audiences (and this will be less easy than for an English production), the whole thing must be comprehensible for non-French speakers. So choose a well-known story and then write the script yourself. You will find nothing published at quite the level you need. Pantomime and fairy story are fruitful areas. My very first attempt at a class play was to have the children act out a poem about the story of St. Nicholas, which I had seen acted out beautifully in a nursery school in Picardie. It was a delightful story for a very young cast to act. Two lost children are cut up by a butcher and put in a barrel, to be rescued miraculously by St. Nicholas. This worked well for the class itself, and brought forth some wonderful French speaking and acting, but was useless as entertainment for the rest of the school, because no-one could understand what was going on! I resolved to choose a 'universal' story next time.

Good publicity for the modern languages department

Apart from the fun of it, it is good publicity for the modern languages department to be seen actually speaking a foreign language in front of the school (and parents). It is also a great confidence booster for the actors. However, it is wise to start with a small play by the class, for the class. This is how I first began, with not the slightest intention of going public. The children were very keen to perform again, but their pleas fell on deaf ears. Then a colleague asked if her class could watch it one wet Friday afternoon and I could not say no. Word got around, as word does, and along came other classes, clamouring. My Head of Year asked if it could be performed in assembly and there we were, dragged shrieking into the limelight.

Don't forget the begging and pleading

The small class play has a special flavour of its own and is well worth doing in its own right. It is easier for the fainthearted to take part in, and is altogether less stressful than a school production. But be prepared – if it is any good at all, the class will want to show it to others. But do not give in too quickly. A certain amount of begging and pleading on their part is essential, in order to increase commitment. After some time, agree to one performance only, in assembly. Later, take it as far as it deserves to go (full school performance one lunch time, parents' evening, ticket performance for outsiders for charity, etc.) Placing the responsibility squarely on them, I usually say 'We'll see if it's good enough', and then, after the first performance: 'Do you think it was good enough?' It has to be their decision. As a result of all this uncertainty, they strive to improve every aspect, and funnily enough, it always *is* good enough in the end …

The self-writing script

You have to write your own script because only you know the character, and the speaking ability, of the performers available to you. It must be an ongoing thing, allowing both for changes of cast and for acting ability. You may have in mind a delightfully romantic speech for the fairy godmother, but find yourself with a rather shy actress, who can only manage a couple of lines. Or you may find Cinderella's father, a minor part, is a talented linguist and actor, and be delighted to write him reams of new lines. A real talent for comedy will often be found in the most surprisingly quiet and reserved people. Give them more to do. In this way, the play almost writes itself. Make the most of the children's own ideas for drama and comedy. Incorporate them all as you go along. They are usually superb.

Don't lose sleep over it

Older and less able classes lack commitment and tend to float in and out of productions, so be flexible. If you have a very temperamental class, don't give up. If Cinderella walks out, don't press her to stay, find another. People who step in to save the day are almost always better performers than those they replace. They tend to be children who are slow to come forward, but very capable. Even if you had somehow suspected their talent you would never have been able to persuade them to take part in the ordinary way. Rescuing the production may be the only way in which they feel able to join in. And what a wonderful opportunity for the retiring to show what they can do. So keep casting fluid, and don't lose sleep over it. (You could easily turn out to be the most nerve-racked of all the participants.)

What to do when the worst happens

Sometimes your worst fears will be realised. Don't despair and don't panic. If your leading player throws a tantrum and refuses to go on on opening night, don't worry. Take to the stage yourself and make a dramatic speech about the reliable child who is coming to the rescue, walking through the part, with the lines in her/his hand. (For once this is a speech that has to be made by you and not one of the children. This may be because only you can fully comprehend and communicate the enormity of the calamity, not to mention the incredible nobility of the one who saves the day.) What a moment of glory for that child, and also for the rest of the cast, who will usually rise magnificently to the occasion and work hard, as a team, to support the newcomer. Both audience and cast will love the drama of it all.

Forget the casting couch

Arriving at a cast is quite an art. It would be a mistake to select one yourself. You need the class to feel the play is 'theirs', not 'yours', thus giving it their full commitment. So from the start, cast only with volunteers. This makes the play a co-operative venture, fully owned by the class. If more than one person wants the same part, hold a simple two-line audition in English (if they aren't any good in English, they won't be any good in French). Then have a class vote. Children are quite good at knowing what parts they can play, and if they are not, the others will soon let them know. Write a part for all who want one, even if it is only two words, and have some non-speaking roles for the shy. As for the shy who are too shy to appear at all, do not pressure them. Give them the vital work of looking after props, costumes, curtain raising, producing programmes, music etc. If you decide the play is good enough, have tickets, with proceeds to charity. This will provide lots of front-of-house work for non-performers. Incidentally, there is something you may not know until you have produced a few French plays of your own. So I will enlighten you now. The most important job of all is the job of *prompter*. Try and resist the urge to do it yourself.

If your actors cannot be heard, forget the whole thing

Because the play is in a foreign language, there may be extra problems with audibility. This is a big issue with all school productions, and you must find a way round it before you even begin. This is the only way I have found to deal with it myself. Be firm. Be very firm. From the first moment anyone opens his or her mouth, don't let them speak unless you can hear them from the back of the hall. Have people standing there to let you know. Just shake your head and tell them you can't hear.

Some will get the hang of it straight away, some have to do a few repeats, but some will take a very long time indeed. You have to be patient with the very shy or low-voiced children. Just go on making them repeat until they speak loudly or become thoroughly fed up and give up. In this case ask them to come back later. After listening to the general volume of the others, they usually find themselves able to join in in the end. If not, give them a two-word or a non-speaking part. Nothing kills a school play faster than inaudibility.

Audibility is not the only problem

To help audibility and memorisation, give everyone their lines and stage directions on a card, written hugely, and in their own colour. Never give anyone the whole typed script. If they have many scenes and many lines, give them many cards. No expectation that the cards will be phased out before the performance will be needed. They will do that automatically. However, there is always one child, sometimes excellent in the part, who, after all the coaching possible from teacher and fellow actors, cannot actually get her mouth round the French. All the help she receives makes no difference, yet she is very keen to keep the part. In these cases, I have found only one method to keep them on the stage. Use phonetics. Give them a card with their lines written as if they were in English. This is not a method I would use in any other circumstances, but it seems to be the only thing that will work for these children. You will worry, as I did, about the impossibility of rendering the soft 'j' or the rolled 'r' using English spelling. That is because you are a teacher, trained in detail. Instead, try to be just a producer of a small play, and decide whether it is better for this child to render his speech imperfectly, or not at all.

How to avoid a nervous breakdown

For those who have not yet produced a play, I am going to pass on a small point of logistics which can only be learnt from harsh experience. It is this: use only one class for your production. If an all-year spectacular seems like a good idea, believe me, it isn't. Arranging out-of-class rehearsals is a nightmare. (It's got to be out-of-class because most other members of staff will be reluctant to give up children for French rehearsals, even for a final dress rehearsal.) Rehearsal times will clash with almost everything else the children do, especially football. You may appear at the appointed hour, but the whole cast will not. There will always be someone missing, often half of them. It happened to me once that only Snow White appeared to rehearse. All right, I thought, what a good opportunity to work with her on her lines. The next rehearsal consisted of a cast of three dwarfs. Now three dwarfs on their own are a contradiction in terms, and did not please me. I would rather have been sitting in the staffroom drinking tea. But worse was to come – two dwarfs, the huntsman and Snow White's mother! At last, patient nobility deserted me, and I began to question, in a less-than-calm manner, exactly how many lunchtimes would need to be given up by me, and how many by the cast, in order to bring this play up to scratch. So choose yourself a class with whom you have lots of lessons, or best of all, your own pastoral group, so that you always have them when you want them. Of course, you will only spend a small part of lesson time rehearsing, because work must go on, but you will be able to use everyone during those other free moments which crop up, and you will have them all together at the end of lessons or if there is a wet-day indoor lunch-time etc. If the wide-screen epic is a must, e.g. 'the French Revolution', then stage it as a series of individual class tableaux in French with overall English narration.

Go bi-lingual for the big spectacular

If you are worried that your class will not be up to the French speaking, there are many ways around the problem. Use of French can vary according to the age and sophistication of the presenting class, and the subject. Nothing is too diffi-cult to present using a certain amount of French, although you may have to resort to a little English too. Or even a lot of English. For example, in 1989, along with just about the entire world media, I was seized by an irresistible urge. It seemed inadvisable, yet I just had to do it. Yes, you've guessed it. I felt impelled to produce an in-school version of the complete French Revolution! In French of course …

Eat your heart out Cecil B. de Mille

Too ambitious, might be your first reaction. But all things are possible. At first, I sat up late at night attempting to write a French script for the whole thing. On the children's level. In suitable French. It was difficult. It was very difficult. My enthu-siasm waned. Realism set in. I gave up. What would have been the point – no-one would have understood it, or been able to perform it convincingly. So we settled for a production narrated in English, with actors using little bursts of French here and there. In the end, the emphasis turned out to be very much on French tableaux – groups of peasants expressing hunger, groups of haughty royals expressing scorn, and a lavish finale – the execution, complete – yes – with guillotine (height measure borrowed from the PE department plus cardboard blade). There was much compe-tition to make the bloody heads to hold up at the end. It was a big success. No play can be too gory …

If at first you don't succeed, miss it out

Performing in a series of tableaux with different narrators provided the opportunity to use more than one class, which resulted in a mega cross-school spectacular, some-thing I usually avoid. Of course, I could only use classes who came to me for French, where the small amount of rehearsal could be fitted into lessons. This was how the tableaux came into being. But the whole school learnt to sing the Marseillaise. The fact that none of us could quite master the obscure middle bit did not hold us back – we simply missed it out. Even though throughout that period, the world's greatest opera singers and choirs were singing it nightly on television, not a soul noticed.

Singing and waving flags

This is the only way to cope with a school French production – do not strive too much for perfection. Let your motto be, 'if you can't manage it, do the next best thing'. When I first discovered the effect of nerves on English singers of French songs, I almost gave up on the singing altogether. What a loss that would have been. Instead, I discovered the miracle of the tape back-up, which works wonders. We could never have managed the fiendishly difficult Marseillaise without it. If purists tut, let them suggest another way to have a 9 to 13-year-old cast sing the Marseillaise at top volume, whilst marching up and down the school hall waving flags …

A performance of the Comédie Française?

If you are using English as narrative with just a small amount of French, let the French you do use be as short and simple as possible. Do not have one person speaking for more than two lines. Another important way to help audience under-standing is to use bi-lingual words whenever you can, for example: 'Je veux danser avec le Prince!', or 'Imbecile!' Hopefully non-French speakers in the audience then have the opportunity to note that there are similarities between the two languages, and to realise, perhaps for the first time, that the French language is not entirely a mystery. If purists complain that you are 'bastardising' the French language, explain gently that this is not a performance of the Comédie Française. Ask them what will be most enjoyable for those new to the French language: being able to pick out a few words here and there which seem familiar, or sitting through a whole play consisting entirely of gobbledygook? Which experience is likely to create affection for the French language?

'Miroir, miroir sur le mur!'

Another way of making a foreign language more accessible is to use repetition for important words. For example, when the Wicked Queen is telling the Huntsman to take Snow White into the forest, have her repeat 'dans la fôret!' at least twice. Then have him repeat it too, in amazed disbelief (an old pantomime technique which can be very effective). Many children in the school audience picked up 'Miroir, miroir, sur le mur!' because of the number of times it was repeated. It was interesting that I heard these words being repeated around the school afterwards, but never heard 'Blanche-Neige' from anybody. This was rather a puzzle, because, of course, 'Blanche-Neige' had had countless repetitions throughout the play. On the other hand, it is not the easiest of words to pronounce. I take this as an indication of the importance of bi-lingual words in foreign language performance. On the other hand, it may just have been their childhood familiarity with the verse. Perhaps it was a combination of both.

Mime, the great communicator

But perhaps the most potent tool for language-learning, used by all teachers in the classroom, is that of mime. Make sure it is the basis of your script. Neither audience nor cast may understand the words 'Regardez les fleurs!', but they will as soon as Snow White points at them. Similarly, gazing at Snow White's apparently dead body, they will understand for the first time 'Elle est morte!', especially when accompanied by the dwarfs' extravagant weeping and wailing! Of course, learning will be helped by the fact that the story is familiar to them, so they know what to expect. Because they are aware of what is to come, they have more brain cells to devote to listening to the language than to working out exactly what is going on.

Making the play their own

Don't let the play be a teaching task. Mention the last play you produced casually, during break duty one day. (Break duty is the time when *real* communication between teacher and pupil takes place.) Leave it at that, and do not ask them if they would like to perform in one. It must come from them. When the deputation from the whole class comes to you asking if they can 'do one', don't accept the offer until you have negotiated a title together. They will want to do 'Neighbours', or 'Terminator 2', you will want to do a universal story with lots of comedy, suitable for its audience. (Of course an episode of 'Star Wars' could be suitable for a very sophisticated school, but not for many). Confine yourself to pointing out a few possibilities only. For example, if this particular class has a larger than average pool of smallish boys with big personalities, remark that they would make good dwarfs for 'Snow White', but only amongst other ideas. When you have found a story agreeable to both parties, say yes. Auditions must also be independent. French speaking is not crucial at this stage, so make audibility the criteria, and let the class choose the actors. They will generally want the most popular children in the main roles, and it is important to go with this group dynamic. A play with actors chosen by you, on merit, will not be owned by the group. A title chosen by you will also fail to attract the same commitment.

Initial script for Cinderella (mainly French)

The script for Cinderella (see below) is an example of a simple play written for Year 7 children, using as much French as possible. (You will always need a small amount of English in your play to avoid confusion for non-French speaking audiences, e.g. some parents.) I call all scripts 'initial' because they have inevitably to be modified in rehearsal to suit the capabilities of the actor. If you are dealing with a more sophisticated group, you will of course be able to write more sophisticated lines (whilst still considering the parents!). The lines in themselves tell you little about the creation of the play. I use the word 'creation' deliberately. It is a joint project, changing all the time as it grows organically out of what the children bring to it in terms of their own imagination, talent and hard work. The success of one of these plays depends entirely on the action, not on the lines, and the scope is infinite. Snow White and her mother must be touchingly pathetic, the Wicked Queen must be completely over the top, and the dwarfs slapstick and comical, each in his own way. Every member of the cast has to mime as if their life depended on it. Music must be lively and costumes extravagant, colourful or comical – begged, borrowed or made by the children themselves. Sound effects must be stunning – the chimes at midnight for Cinderella, the boy with the booming voice hidden behind the Wicked Queen's mirror etc. Lots of weeping, wailing, laughing, dying, attempted murder, shrieking, singing, dancing, pushing, fighting, terror, hatred, falling over, pathos, loving, and kind nobility have to be added to the script if your production is to be a success. In other words, if it is to be spectacular, extravagant and fun!

Initial script for 'St Joan' (mainly English)

This script (see below) was written for children aged nine to eleven, and quickly became a script with very little French. Perhaps the complexity of the subject somehow led to this result. A series of tableaux in French, narrated overall in English, worked well, without intimidating the children, who gave the battles and the marching about their all. Perhaps this is the best way to present an epic subject. The marching about went down so well that I started to look at the idea of having Joan on some sort of horse (a cardboard head with cloth-draped-over-stick body?). The idea appealed to me instantly. I decided the final scene demanded it ('El Cid' riding into history'?). In fact, the whole play would be a flop without the horse. Because *everyone* knows that St. Joan went everywhere on a big white horse. How peculiar she was going to look trudging along with the soldiers! (How peculiar would she have looked bobbing about on a cardboard horse?) In the end, reason prevailed, and I gave up on the horse. Be aware that you may also suffer from such obsessions (part of the creative process?), and know where to draw the line. Know when to say no to yourself. I truly believe that if anyone had offered me a real horse, I would have jumped at it, with consequences not difficult to imagine!

Guillotining is easier than burning at the stake

The 'burning at the stake' scene also presented a problem. The guillotine scene in our 'French Revolution' went off very well. We were able to successfully execute the king and queen in a ritualistic sort of way, using cardboard cut-out heads and drums, which didn't seem appropriate for the execution of Joan. It was difficult to decide what to do. There seemed to be five options:

(1)   do not to include it at all;
(2)   hint at it;
(3)   describe it whilst it happens off-stage (shades of Racine!);
(4)   act it out ritualistically;
(5)   act it out realistically (but not *too* realistically!)

Despite the importance of the event, and the dramatic opportunity it presented, in the end I decided (not 'we' this time – young people can be very bloodthirsty), to gloss the whole thing over with a quick mention 'en passant', as it were, and hasten on to the final scene. (Could the PE department rise to the construction of a suitably large bonfire? Of course the children would have been only too happy to oblige, but then what would we have done with it?). I was also torn over the use of 'burnt alive' (twice), considering substituting 'executed' instead, which would be an option for a very young class. Only you can really know how far to go with scenes like these, because only you really know your actors and your audience. It is true that young people are familiar with the most grisly scenes on television and video, from a very young age. But what can be done in the school hall, perhaps in front of parents, has nothing to do with what can be done on television and video.

Script for 'Carl's Christmas Catastrophe' (totally English)

Of course an entertaining piece about France does not have to be in French at all, mainly or otherwise. For a quick scene on something like the Christmas concert, anything is possible. (Although I must admit I have always liked the idea of doing a French nativity). 'Carl's Christmas Catastrophe' (see below) was written with a particular boy in mind. His acting is vital. Only a giant personality could carry it off. He *was* a giant personality, plus a rather naughty boy, which made him totally credible in the part. Narrators must also have lots of acting talent. (The upper case words are for them, to indicate emphasis). The original idea was to have questions for the audience at the end, such as 'Where does Santa Claus put the presents in France?' or 'What do they eat instead of Christmas pudding?', but we decided to drop them in the end, as not in keeping with the fun of the thing. Perhaps more appropriate for an assembly?

Don't forget assembly

Assemblies are an excellent opportunity for raising the profile of the modern languages department. You can have an assembly about almost any aspect of language learning. To start with, two for each trip or visit – the pre-trip assembly and the post-trip assembly. Something about Christmas in France or elsewhere, and at least a foreign language carol for the carol concert. If there is something topical going on abroad which the children are genuinely interested in, do an assembly about it. My best ever was on the subject of the Channel Tunnel, partly because we had booked our day trip crossing on it. Of course the trippers were most interested. (Unfortunately our booking was cancelled, so we made the trip by ferry as usual. But we got to know a lot about the Channel Tunnel.) A middle school can delight the lower school children when they come up for their preliminary visit to the school, with a presentation of first French songs. These lend themselves particularly well to comedy, e.g. sleeping monk suddenly attacked by someone with large pillow, cross bird hopping about having successive parts of its anatomy plucked, people demonstrating how to plant cabbages with their elbow. The visitors don't know what's going on but they get the message that French is fun!

Choose the loud but execrable

Schools are multicultural these days and it seems churlish not to recognise that there are other languages spoken there in addition to those which are taught. For the harvest festival, you can organise a contribution from those languages without being able to speak them yourself. The secret is to keep it simple. Find one or two children for each language who will bring something in and present it with a brief word like 'I'm bringing flowers' in their mother tongue. Some may find it difficult to bring anything in, so always have a few apples in reserve on the day, for the sake of 'international relations'. (It's important to have all the languages up there. In the most ethnically mixed school I taught in we could usually count on French, Italian, Urdu, Punjabi, Hindi and Bengali.) If you have any particularly fluent speakers (we often had very fluent Italians), let them do a prayer, with a simultaneous translation in English so that the audience can appreciate similarities between the two languages. Have the main prayers in French, with or without translation. What you do and how you do it will depend entirely on the speakers at your disposal, but here's a tip. If you have to choose between readers for the French prayer who are quiet, totally competent, and whose French is excellent, and a couple of rogues who are loud, totally confident and whose French is execrable, don't hesitate. Choose the loud but execrable. In my experience, they are impervious to nerves, perform with supreme conviction, and nobody notices the pronunciation. In any case, for some reason you will never find performers like this with good spoken French. And they do wonders for the prestige of the department, as everyone asks themselves how on earth you managed to get them up there *speaking French*!

The crippling of the modern languages department

If your school has an annual Staff Concert, beware. I have had only two brushes with this concept, both disastrous. For the first, the entire staff of the modern languages department opted for a performance of the can-can, with authentic bloomers. We were not exactly middle-aged, but slightly past the first flush of youth, as you might say, and for this reason started rehearsals in good time. Exactly how far past the first flush of youth we actually were, we realised after only a couple of bars. We called for slower music. We thought of giving up. We thought of taking early retirement. But it was too late. We were famous already, and the whole school was buzzing with anticipation of this amazing sight. We were the high spot of the whole show. Our pride as a department was at stake. We had to continue. We practised every day, wearing ourselves out in the hope of becoming fitter. Maybe we did, but we still were not fit enough. Then there were *three performances* (I really thought I might have a heart-attack), after which no-one could walk properly for a week. Our only saving grace was that one of our troupe could do the splits and raise a cheer at the end.

Think twice about your Edith Piaf impersonation

Needless to say there was no repeat performance. Until a few years later and the advent of younger members of staff. I had no difficulty in declining the invitation to take part this time, but I wanted to be in the production, so decided to paint a black beard on my face, borrow a man's black suit and top hat, and sew two shoes cut in half onto the front of my trouser legs. During the performance I had to hang around watching the dancers do their routine, on my knees. Of course, I don't need to tell you who I was impersonating, but it was a part which was totally unappreciated by the whole of the school. Far from being lost in admiration, not one person congratulated me on my superb performance, not a single class asked me how I did it, or said I looked good in a beard, not even my own class. I had been sure I could rely on them to admire the ingenuity of the shoes (secretly cut in half in the Craft, Design and Technology department, no less), or to ask me why I was walking on my knees. I began to feel a total failure. Had it been so unremarkable, after all my efforts? I became depressed. After a week had passed by, I swallowed my pride and asked a pupil what she had thought of my performance. It turned out that no-one had the faintest idea that I had been in the play. Worse, no-one knew who the eccentric person in the black beard and top hat, lurking on his knees, was meant to be! After this humiliation and disappointment, I quit the boards forever. The moral of this story is: think twice before you bring out your Edith Piaf impersonation!

The Story of Cinderella

1. We would like to present the story of Cinderella.
2. On vous présente l'histoire de Cendrillon.

1. Scene 1: Cinderella's mother

2. La mere de Cendrillon

A. Cinderella was a happy little girl.

B. Until one day:

Maman:	Cendrillon! Cendrillon!
Cendr:	(enters, skipping) Oui, Maman?
Maman:	Bonjour, Cendrillon, ma petite.
Cendr:	Bonjour, Maman. (kiss)
Maman:	Voilà, ma chérie! (gives parcel)
Cendr:	Qu'est-ce que c'est, Maman?
Maman:	C'est un livre, ma petite.
Cendr:	(opens and examines) Ah, c'est un livre fantastique! Merci, Maman. (sits and reads) J'adore ça … (Sit for a while reading. Mother dies)
Cendr:	Maman! Maman! Papa! Papa! Viens vite! Viens vite! (enter Papa, looks at wife)
Papa:	Elle est morte!!!!!
Cendr:	Elle est morte? Ah, non! Maman n'est pas morte!
Papa:	Oui, ma petite, elle est morte … (both cry in each others' arms) (body carried off)

1. Scene 2: New sisters for Cinderella

2. Nouvelles soeurs pour Cendrillon

A. Soon Cinderella's father found a new wife, with three beautiful daughters of her own.

Papa:	Je t'adore, ma pomme de terre! Embrasse-moi!
B-mere:	Je t'adore, mon chou-fleur! Embrasse-moi! (they run towards each other and miss)
Cendr:	(enter, surprised) Papa, qui est-ce?
Papa:	C'est une nouvelle maman pour toi.
Cendr:	(shocked) Une nouvelle maman? Pour moi?
B-mere:	Qui est-ce, mon amour?
Papa:	C'est ma petite fille, Cendrillon.
B-mere:	(Steps back) Quelle horreur!
Cendr:	Bonjour, Maman. (curtsies)
B-mere:	Elle n'est pas belle, ta fille. Elle est horrible. Regardez *mes* enfants! J'ai trois filles ravissantes. (calls them on) Mauricette! Polycette! Marionnette! (kisses them) Elles sont adorables!
Papa:	Je vous présente ma fille, Cendrillon. (they draw back, mother kicks them so they shake hands with Cendrillon, pretending to be sick at the same time)

Soeurs:	Yuk!
Maur:	Je suis la plus belle!
Poly:	Non! Je suis la plus belle! (pushes Maur. aside)
Mar:	Non, non, non! Je suis la plus belle! (they fight)
B-mere:	Taisez-vous, mes enfants! Taisez-vous! (she chases them off with a big stick)

1. *Scene 3: The wonderful dress*
2. *La robe merveilleuse.*

A.   Soon the prince decided to give a ball.
B.   He was looking for a wife.
A.   Mauricette, Polycette and Marionette were sure he would choose them.
B.   Cendrillon was invited too, but her stepmother would not allow her to go.
A.   Here they are getting ready for the ball.

B-mere:	(crossly) Cendrillon!
Maur:	(crossly) Cendrillon!
Poly:	(crossly) Cendrillon!
Mar:	(crossly) Cendrillon!
B-mere:	Cendrillon! Tu as fini?
Cendr:	(carrying in some hideous shoes) Non, Maman.
B-mere:	(slaps her) Idiote!
Maur:	Ma robe, Cendrillon! Imbécile!
Poly:	Mes cheveux, Cendrillon! Crétine!
Mar:	Mon sac, Cendrillon! Stupide! (C. cries)
B-mere:	Vous êtes si belles, mes enfants!
Maur:	Je suis la plus belle!
Poly:	Je suis la plus belle!
Mar:	Je suis la plus belle! (they begin to push and shove)
B-mere:	Taisez-vous!
Cendr:	Maman, s'il vous plaît …
B-mere:	Silence, stupide!
Cendr:	Je voudrais aller au bal!
B-mere:	Tu voudrais aller au bal? Toi? (all laugh)
Cendr:	Oui, s'il vous plaît.
B-mere:	Tu as une robe?
Cendr:	Non, maman.
B-mere:	Alors! (all laugh)
Soeurs:	Elle voudrait aller au bal! C'est ridicule! C'est impossible! Elle est trop laide! (they put on their things and leave; C. stays behind, crying)
Cendr:	Je voudrais aller au bal, et danser avec le prince (enter fairy godmother)
B-fee:	Qu'est-ce que tu veux, ma petite?
Cendr:	Mais qui êtes-vous, madame?

B-fee:	Je suis ta bonne fée. (waves wand)
Cendr:	Ma bonne fée?
B-fee:	Oui, ma petite, je suis ta bonne fée. Qu'est-ce que tu désires?
Cendr:	Je voudrais aller au bal danser avec le prince!
B-fee:	Tres bien, ma petite. Tu vas aller au bal. Tu vas danser avec le prince! (waves wand)
Cendr:	Mais, je ne peux pas, bonne fée.
B-fee:	Tu ne peux pas, ma petite? Mais pourqoi pas?
Cendr:	Je n'ai pas de robe! Je ne suis pas belle!
B-fee:	Mais Cendrillon, tu es la *plus* belle! Et je te donnerai une robe merveilleuse!
Cendr:	Une robe merveilleuse?
B-fee:	Oui, une robe merveilleuse. Et tu seras la plus belle. Et tu vas danser avec le prince. (begins to exit but leads C. back to front stage). Ecoute, ma chérie. A minuit, tu dois rentrer à la maison.
Cendr:	A minuit? Pourquoi?
B-fee:	Parce que … écoute … à minuit tout sera fini!
Cendr:	Tout sera fini?
B-fee:	(nods) Tout.
Cendr:	Et la robe merveilleuse?
B-fee:	Oui, la robe merveilleuse sera fini.
Cendr:	Je comprends. A minuit, je dois rentrer à la maison.
B-fee:	Tres bien. Viens, ma chérie. (leads C. off)

1. Scene 4: Cinderella at the ball

2. Cendrillon au bal

A. So Cinderella did go to the ball.

B. And nobody knew who she was.

A. Especially not her stepmother and her 3 daughters. (enter stepmother and daughters. They look round)

B-mere:	Où est le prince?
Soeurs:	Où est le prince? Ou est-il? Il n'est pas là!
Invites:	Je ne sais pas. (sisters scuffle and generally make a nuisance of themselves)
B-mere:	Taisez-vous! Taisez-vous! (she gets a stick out of her bag looks around and then puts it away again) (enter C.)
Invites:	Qui est-ce? Je ne sais pas. Elle est belle! Quelle robe merveilleuse! Elle est si belle!
Soeurs:	Je suis la plus belle, etc. (push and shove)
B-mere:	Taisez-vous!
Valet:	Silence! Silence pour Son Altesse Royal, le Prince Charmant! (enter prince, looks at all guests, chooses C. to dance with) (ugly sisters sob loudly)

B-mere:	Taisez-vous! (all dance)
Prince:	(kneels in front of C.) Mademoiselle, je vous aime, je vous aime. Voulez-vous me marier? (clock strikes twelve midnight)
Cendr:	Ah! Il est minuit! Tout sera fini! (runs away, leaving shoe. All run after. Footman picks up shoe)
Prince:	Mademoiselle! Mademoiselle! Je vous aime! (the ugly sisters dance round in a circle with glee)

1. Scene 5: le prince trouve sa princesse
2. The prince finds his princess

A. The prince searched for C. everwhere.
B. He swore that he would marry the girl whose foot would fit the lost shoe.
A. In rags again, C. worked in the kitchen.

Cendr:	Mon prince, mon prince … (sighs) je t'aime, je t'aime …
B-mere:	(enters and gives C. a bucket). Voila! Dépêchez-vous, idiote!
Soeurs:	(rush in falling over each other) Le prince! Le prince!
B-mere:	Le prince est ici?
Soeurs:	Le prince est ici!
B-mere:	(tidies them up, looks at C.) Quelle horreur! Papa! Papa! (enter papa) Papa, sortez avec Cendrillon! Vite, vite!
Papa:	Sortez, mon amour? Mais pourquoi?
B-mere:	Pourquoi? Parce qu'elle est ridicule! (all laugh. Papa and C. are pushed out by the ugly sisters. Enter prince and retinue, with the shoe on a cushion)
Soeurs:	Je suis la plus belle etc. (pushing and shoving, they try on the shoe with great difficulty)
Prince:	C'est tout?
Soeurs:	Oui, oui, c'est tout. (prince looks round sadly and turns to go)
Papa:	(bursts in) Attendez, mon prince, attendez! Regardez ma fille, Cendrillon! (he pulls C. on, she is ashamed of her rags) Viens, ma petite, viens!
B-mere:	Quelle horreur!
Soeurs:	(pointing) Elle est stupide! Elle est ridicule! Elle est laide!
Prince:	(leads C. front stage and kneels in front of her) Cendrillon, mon amour. Je vous aime. Voulez-vous me marier? Voulez-vous être ma princesse?
Cendr:	(cannot believe it) Oh, oui, mon prince. (they kiss, all applaud, except:)
B-mere:	Cendrillon, une princesse? Ce n'est pas possible!
Soeurs:	(repeat, sobbing)
Prince:	Je vous presente Cendrillon, ma princesse! (leads her off) (stepmother faints, ugly sisters sob etc.)

A. And so Cinderella married the prince and they both lived happily ever after. Au revoir!

The Story of Joan of Arc

1. We would like to present the story of Joan of Arc.
2. On vous presente l'histoire de Jeanne d'Arc.

1. Scene 1: France in 1414

2. La France en quatorze-cent quatorze

A.   500 years ago the King of England wanted to become the King of France. (soldiers march into the hall from back)

B.   English soldiers were marching through France. (stop front)

A.   They captured Paris. (hold up card 'Paris')

B.   They captured Reims. (hold up card 'Reims')

A.   They captured Orleans. (hold up card 'Orleans')

B.   All the great cities and forts of France were in their hands. ('France is ours! France is ours!') ('La France est à nous! La France est à nous!') (march off)

1. Scene 2: At the court of King Charles

2. A la cour du roi Charles

A.   Charles, the French king, was very frightened. (worry, pace)

B.   He had not even been crowned properly, because the English had captured the coronation cathedral at Reims.

A.   Now he was running out of money and men to fight with. (look in chest, shake head)

B.   He asked his nobles to help him. (Donne-moi de l'argent! Donne-moi des soldats!)

A.   But they would not. ('Non. non! Je ne veux pas!') ('Absolument pas!') ('Je n'ai pas d'argent!')

B.   Some even left Charles and went to join the English. (exit half nobles) ('Adieu, votre Majesté!') (Adieu, votre Majesté!) (Adieu, Votre Majesté!)

A.   They wanted to be on the winning side.

1. Scene 3: in the village of Domremy

2. Au village de Domremy

A.   All this time, a little girl in the village of Domremy had been looking after her father's sheep.

B.   Her name was Jeanne d'arc - we know her as Joan of Arc. (wander)

A   One day, when she was thirteen, out in the fields, St Margaret appeared to her in a vision. (rub eyes)

B.   She said: 'Joan, God has chosen you to do a great work. You must save France!' ('Jeanne, sauve la France!')

A.   Joan did not understand. How could a young girl save France? ('Je suis une petite fille!') (exit St Margaret)

B.   The next day Saint Catherine appeared before her.

51

A.   She told Joan that God wanted her to have Charles crowned in Reims cathedral. ('Jeanne, sauve la France!)

B.   Joan was horrified. How on earth could she do such a thing? ('Moi, sauve la France? Je ne peux pas!)

A.   For three years Joan went on hearing the voices of St Margaret and St Catherine. (saints enter and exit)

B.   She told nobody.

A.   But more and more, she knew she must obey them.

1. Scene 4: Joan tells her father

2. Jeanne parle à son pere

A.   When she was sixteen, Joan told her father about her voices.

B.   She told him that God had chosen her to save France.

A.   Her mother cried:

Jeanne: 'Maman, je dois sauver la France!'

Mere: 'Ah, non, Jeanne! Ce n'est pas possible!'

B.   Her sisters laughed:

Jeanne: 'Nicolette, Marianne, je dois sauver la France!'

Soeurs: 'C'est ridicule!' 'Hee hee hee!' 'Idiote!'

A.   Her father said he would rather drown her with his own hands than let her go off with soldiers:

Jeanne: 'Papa, je dois sauver la France!'

Papa: 'Que je vais te jeter dans la rivière avant!' (exit Jeanne in tears)

1. Scene 5: a visit to the French army

2. Visite à l'armée française

A.   Joan crept away and went to see the nearest French army commander, Robert de Baudricourt.

B.   She asked him to take her to see the king.

A.   He told her to go home at once, where her father should give her a good whipping.

Robert: Ridicule jeune fille! Rentre a la maison! Qu'est-ce que ton père va dire?

A.   But Joan did not give up. She kept on hearing her voices and talking about her mission, although her father beat her.

B.   A year later, she ran away to see Robert de Baudricourt again.

A.   By this time, the French army was desperate.

B.   He was ready to consider anything which might help defeat the English.

A.   She convinced him to let her go.

Jeanne: (kneeling) 'Je dois sauver la France. Je dois aller voir le roi!'

Robert: 'Très bien, ma fille. Allons voir le roi. Viens avec moi.'

B.   He gave Joan the clothes of a soldier.

Robert: 'Voilà, Jeanne'.

Jeanne: 'Merci beaucoup, monsieur.'
A.   The people of the town brought her a horse.
Citoyen: 'Voilà, Jeanne. Et bonne chance!'
Jeanne: 'Merci beaucoup.'
B.   Robert de Baudricourt gave her a sword, saying: 'Go, and let come what may!
A.   And so Joan rode away from her village, ready to save France.

1. Scene 6: At the court of King Charles
2. A la cour du roi Charles
A.   Charles and his nobles were surprised to hear about this young peasant girl
    who thought she could save France.
B.   They decided to set her a test, to see if God really had sent her.
A.   When Joan arrived, Charles changed places with one of his nobles and a noble
    sat on his throne.
B.   Would Joan be able to pick him out?
Jeanne: (going straight to the king) 'Sire, je m'appelle Jeanne d'arc. Je dois sauver
    la France'. (kneels and kisses his hand)
A.   Now Charles was sure Joan had been sent by God to help him.
B.   With new hope, he buckled on his sword.
A.   And the army, with Joan at its head, rode out to defeat the English …

1. Scene 7: The battle of Orleans
2. La bataille d'Orleans
A.   First they rode to Orleans. (hold up card)
B.   The English were frightened when they saw an army led by a girl! (English
    soldiers stop front)
A.   Nothing could stop the French soldiers. (fight)
B.   By nightfall, they had taken Orleans and driven the English army out. (fight)
A.   They marched on to other forts and cities and drove the English out of all of
    them.
B.   They believed that Joan had been sent by God to save their country.
A.   Finally they came to Reims, the coronation city. (hold up card)
B.   They drove the English out forever.

1. Scene 8: Charles is crowned at Reims
2. Charles est couronné roi à Reims
A.   Joan led Charles into the cathedral at Reims.
B.   It was her last victory.
A.   With tears in her eyes, she stood by as he was crowned King of France.
Charles: 'Merci, Jeanne d'arc'.
Jeanne: 'Vive le roi! Vive le roi!'

B.   Now she begged him to let her go back to her home in the country, to look after her sheep again.

Jeanne: 'Sire, je veux rentrer à mes moutons!'

Charles: 'Non, non! Tu dois continuer à mener mon armée!'

A.   But Joan's work was done.

B.   She could not hear her voices any more. (enter saints)

Ste. Cath:'Adieu, Jeanne'.

Ste Marg:'Adieu, Jeanne'.

Jeanne: 'Ne me quittez pas! Ne me quittez pas!' (she weeps)

1. Scene 9: Joan is betrayed

2. Jeanne est trahie

A.   Some of Charles' nobles were secretly on the English side. They would do anything to stop him winning the war.

B.   They decided that the only way to prevent this was to get rid of Joan.

A.   During battle, they handed her over to the enemy for 10,000 gold pieces.

1. Scene 10: Joan in prison

2. Jeanne en prison

A.   Joan was taken by the English and thrown into a dark dungeon.

B.   For three years, they tried to make her confess that she was a witch.

A.   They wanted her to say that she had been sent by the devil.

B.   They told her she would be burnt alive if she did not confess.

A.   But Joan would not.

B.   In May, 1431, she was burnt alive in the town square of Rouen.

A.   She was 19 years old.

1. Scene 11: Saint Joan

2. Sainte Jeanne

A.   Many years later, she was made a saint by the French church.

B.   May 30th was is set aside every year in memory of the peasant girl

A.   A faithful soldier of Jesus Christ. (Carrying a flag, Joan leads soldiers down from the stage as if into battle, marching through the hall and disappearing at the back).

Carl's Christmas Catastrophe!

1.
Carl met a boy whilst out at play
He said he came from FRENCH CALAIS.
He asked our Carl to come and stay.
'O.K.' said Carl, 'I'm on my way!'

2.
Carl packs his suitcase with no fears
His mother says goodbye with tears:
'Be careful, my own darling boy!'
His father just says: 'Ship ahoy!'

3.
On board the ship Carl settles down
To watch the video in the lounge.
He does not see FRANCE drawing near,
Nor hear the captain shout 'WE'RE HERE!'

4.
The passengers all take their leave;
The captain with one mighty heave,
Pulls up the gangplank very quick.
Now there's no way to LEAVE THE SHIP!

5.
At last Carl looks around to find
He's certainly been LEFT BEHIND!
He grabs his case and makes a run –
He doesn't see the GANGPLANK'S GONE!
(!!!!!! SPLASH !!!!!!)

6.
Then Carl has to make such a swim
He comes out SOAKED right to the skin!
'Welcome to France!' the family say.
Says Pierre: 'Did you swim ALL THE WAY?'

7.
When French folk meet the custom is
To grab each other and PLANT A KISS!
This is their way, they like to share it,
We English have to GRIN AND BEAR IT!

8.
Before he has a chance to run,
Carl's well and truly KISSED BY MUM!

Then 'Quelle horreur!' BY DAD AS WELL!
Carl wonders if he is in hell?
    9.
They hurry home, it's Christmas time
Carl hears the bells of midnight chime.
'We're off the CHURCH, it's Christmas eve!'
Says Pierre, but Carl CANNOT BELIEVE!
    10.
'What? CAROLS NOW?' yells Carl, aghast.
'In England bedtime is long past!'
He won't join in and just SLEEPS FAST,
Through the whole lot, from first to last!
    11.
'What other SILLY CUSTOMS lurk?'
Cries Carl when they get back from church.
Sees all their shoes around the fireplace,
And shrieks, 'This family is a NUTCASE!'
    12.
'Oh, no, my friend', says Pierre, 'you see
Not STOCKINGS HERE, but SHOES will be
Filled up with gifts for you and me.'
'What rot!' sneers Carl, 'you can't FOOL ME!'
    13.
Into the fire the angry boy
Throws BOTH HIS SHOES, just to annoy.
When Santa leaves him NOT ONE TOY,
Carl's cross to see the others' joy.
    14.
Next comes the turkey – what delight!
At last they're doing something right
But woe! Alas! Carl SCOFFS THE LOT!
And then shouts out, 'WHAT PUD YOU GOT?'
    15.
Pierre's brother whispers, 'What a hog!'
Then Mum brings in the CHOCOLATE LOG.
'You stupid people!' Carl calls out,
'I must have CHRISTMAS PUD, look out!'
    16.
In vain poor Pierre explains to him
That it's the French way – CARL'S TOO DIM!

Of chocolate log he takes a spoon
and spits it RIGHT ACROSS THE ROOM!
    17.
The family all cry 'OOH LA LA!'
And father says 'He's gone too far!
He must go!' Pierre cries 'Non, Papa!
Please let him stay, HE'S COME SO FAR!'
    18.
So thinking of the Common Market,
And having cleaned up ALL THE CARPET.
They all agree that Carl can stay,
If only for ANOTHER DAY.
    19.
In January, Carl's been told,
Another party they will hold.
INTO A CAKE Mama will fold
A SPECIAL CHARM which may be gold!
    20.
That day is called THE FEAST OF KINGS.
The special charm great good luck brings.
Whoever finds it in his cake
KING FOR THE DAY the charm will make.
    21.
Carl's desperate to WEAR THE CROWN,
His cake he's really wolfing down.
And soon he's yelling, 'I want more!'
But what's this? Now he's ON THE FLOOR!
    22.
'Don't eat too fast, dear,' says Pierre's Mum,
'I think he's CHOKING ON A CRUMB'.
The family view him with alarm,
Says Pierre, 'I think he's FOUND THE CHARM!
    23.
'I've found the charm! I'VE BEATEN YOU!'
Shrieks Carl, who's turned COMPLETELY BLUE
'I'll fetch the doctor', cries Papa,
And dashes off to get the car.
    24.
Pierre says, 'But, mother, if he chokes
Whatever will we TELL HIS FOLKS?

His sister sobs, his mother cries,
But, SAD TO SAY, our poor Carl dies.
    25.
The doctor rushes in, 'WHAT'S WRONG?'
Carl's celebrations were not long.
'Put him to bed,' the doctor said,
Too late, the FOOLISH BOY WAS DEAD!
    26.
They took his corpse to meet the boat,
With many A SIGH AND GROAN …
Oh, foolish boy! Oh, foolish Carl!
YOU SHOULD HAVE STAYED AT HOME!

Harvest festival

Part 1

Merci à Dieu qui nous donne à manger tous les jours.
1. Merci à Dieu pour le soleil at la pluie.
2. Merci à Dieu pour les fruits et les légumes.
3. Merci à Dieu pour les vaches et les moutons.
4. Merci à Dieu pour les poissons et les poulets.
5. Merci à Dieu pour le lait et le vin.
6. Merci à Dieu pour le pain et les bonbons.
Merci à Dieu qui nous donne à manger tous les jours.

Part 2

1. Moi, j'apporte des pommes.
2. Moi, j'apporte des poires.
3. Moi, j'apporte des bananes.
4. Moi, j'apporte des haricots verts.
5. Moi, j'apporte des pommes de terre.
6. Moi, j'apporte des oranges.
7. Moi j'apporte du pain

Part 3

Repeat Part 1

Chapter 7

The importance of the visual

Q Is it just a time-filler?
Q Are display boards worth the effort?
Q How to acquire materials (authentic or unauthentic)
Q Can you succeed as an IT expert?
A The more visual, the more meaningful for learning
A Have helpers in order to avoid display fatigue
A Go abroad with a big suitcase, have a friend abroad, or be imaginative at home
A Use the expertise which is around you

Never underestimate your own duck

As we all know, but sometimes forget, learning involves more than simply listening and remembering. Some teachers teach as if that were the case, and are startlingly unsuccessful in their efforts. In fact, our brain is programmed to learn visually, as well as aurally. At any age. Hence the more graphic your lessons can be, the more meaningful they are to the learner. We can all remember things we have seen years ago, when we have long forgotten what we have heard. Learning a language in the country where it is spoken is a visual as well as an aural process, the spoken prompt often accompanied by the visual. Your hostess offers you chicken whilst holding out the dish. Language teachers strive to reproduce similar conditions in the classroom, using flashcards, role-play etc. Artwork and display has a major part to play. Maximum use should be made of colour. 'Colour is one of the most powerful tools for enhancing memory and creativity.'[1] Looking at a brightly coloured picture of a duck on the wall with 'le canard' written underneath, is a spur to memorisation. Looking at a picture of a duck drawn by your friend in his own idiosyncratic way, is an even better spur. Looking at a picture of a duck drawn painstakingly by *yourself* is the best spur of all.

Autonomy and self-expression

We have all heard the story of the boy who informed his new and eager French teacher that: 'I don't do French, Miss, I do colouring'! Desperate language teachers of less-than-interested pupils have been driven to this strategy when confronted by the totally alienated more often than anyone cares to admit. It is a strategy which will not be needed in a class where everyone is learning at their own pace and feels in control of that learning. But a learner who chooses to produce a visual aid to memory for general display is using more than his artistic skills. He is developing the skill of independent learning, satisfying his need for autonomy, expressing the natural urge to excel, and the equally important desire to belong to the group and to help others within that community. In all these ways he is improving his self-esteem.

Let them choose

As a person of very minor artistic talent, I have been amazed at the vibrant beauty and creativity of the work many pupils produce for display on a regular basis. The secret is, I think, that they have chosen what they do. No-one is ever *told* to make a poster of cow for the wall. It is not compulsory. They have selected that particular animal from many others because of associations it has for them. When the art master, seeing French posters etc. on corridor display boards, signed by the artist, asked me what I did to get such work out of certain children, I did not have a reply. I did nothing. Lend a felt-tip pen occasionally? Ensure that nothing mediocre reached the wall? (The mediocre poster will remain in the folder, not unappreciated – it has served its purpose – but just failing to reach the very high standard required for display.) Oh, and ensuring of course that the finished piece of work is treated with the respect it deserves, will be recognised, valued and displayed with care. (Sometimes not happening in schools where teachers suffer from overload). That is the limit of my input.

Involve them all

I have never seen artwork as the province of the very young learner. People with artistic ability seek to express it throughout their life. A GCSE class of mine agreed to help out with an open day for the lower schools coming up the following year, by making a French alphabet frieze. We decided that an as-far-as-possible bilingual frieze would be the most welcoming and I supplied any unfamiliar vocabulary needed. Had we had more time to devote to the project they could have done the whole thing themselves, but exam pressure meant no time to do the work in class. Of course, artwork done at home is always less reliable. Not every volunteer produced the perfect picture, with perfect lettering. (You must have a rule about lettering. Children who will devote hours to creating a picture may consider the writing element unworthy. They may dash off an insignificant, even indecipher-able, scrawl. A poster without a large clear caption is of no value whatsoever for language learning. Stipulate a minimum height for letters and teach bubble writing to those in difficulty. It's the only way.) With work undertaken at home, expect to have disappointments and failures to produce what was promised: regard it as inevitable (it's that budgie again). Don't worry. Keener people will step in to save the day and will not let the thing founder. The frieze looked sensational when it went up and was admired for months. The artists enjoyed it and the incoming children enjoyed it. Valuable lessons in communal responsibility were also learnt, particularly by those who failed to produce as promised.

Use the corridor

Display work in the classroom helps with learning and is a source of pride and pleasure to its creators. In addition, it has another function – in the corridor. Corridor displays are especially important. Their purpose is to enhance the prestige of your subject. If it is well done, which means interesting enough to attract the attention of the passer-by, good display work gives the foreign language a physical presence in the school. In order to do this successfully the standard must be high, and practical preparation undertaken. First, acquire your boards. Corridor display boards may be in great demand in your establishment and you may have to fight for them. On the other hand, they may be generally unwanted and you may have to fight *not* to have them.

The vandalism trap

Take on only as many as you can maintain properly in the time you have. I worked in a school where staff were not interested in display boards. Many of them were empty. Concerned by an imminent inspection, the Head decided to allocate a certain number of boards to each teacher, to be kept full at all times. He wanted all the boards to be used, and hoped in this way to cheer up his bare corridors. Unfortunately, uninterested board-owners could think of nothing to fill them with but drab and uninteresting material. Having done so, they could never find the time to renew it. Ever. The display, never attractive in the first place, was soon in tatters. Neglected boards look even worse than empty boards and are an invitation to vandalism. If your display work is really attractive and of interest, it is less likely to be damaged. Start with just a couple of boards if you are not sure how you are going to fill them.

Is there life after Blutack?

Your carefully chosen work will not pack any sort of punch if it is displayed on dilapidated boards. If yours are shabby ask to have them painted, and if this fails (as it might), cover them with bright paper – strong colours, not pale. Dark colours show off the work at its best. If you are still attached to that unmentionable board-covering material of all our youths, whose name I hardly dare mention here lest it stir up long-forgotten cravings in some who were recovered years ago, I will just give the initials: S.P.(!) Yes, I'm afraid so. All schools in the past were run on the stuff. It had an unmistakable misty, wishy-washy tint in whatever colour it proposed itself to be, even black. But it mostly came in strangely vague colours like computer grey, eyeball yellow, corpse beige and greenish white. It came in liberal supplies when nothing else did, and once applied to the boards it disintegrated with the speed of rice paper. (Maybe it *was* rice paper.) I apologise for bringing up the subject, but if you are still a user please get help. (Samaritans will give you the number of an excellent 'Ten Steps' group for coming off S.P.) Staple everything – Blutack creates mess and is mysteriously pulled off, leaving nasty stains. It also tends to wreck the work when the time comes for it to be taken down and returned to its owners. Borrow, or otherwise acquire a staple remover at all costs. As I see it, really good work being torn down and crushed into the bin, like rubbish, is the easy way out, and not treating the effort which went into that work with the respect which it deserves. Taking down with care is indeed more time-consuming, but it is a task which can be delegated.

Display board fatigue sets in early

Covering boards is another time-consuming and irritating task. I find it irritating because it has to be done so often. It seems that no sooner is your gorgeous, pristine coloured paper glowing up on the walls, than it is ready to come down again, suffering from the myriad small defects paper is heir to – fading, scuffs, little tears, holes, dirty marks, coming loose, wet patches, I could go on … For the sake of your sanity, train up a couple of willing helpers to cover the boards for you. Sometimes people who are not too keen on the playground will be happy to spend wet breaks inside doing this. I say 'train up' because this is a skilled job, for which they will need a certain amount of manual dexterity. Training to take work down without damaging the backing paper can also be successful, but training to put *up* work is much more problematic. Depending on the type of school you are in, you my have to retain this task for yourself. It seems to be one of those things volunteers don't do well. Once you have trained your pair, stick to them like glue. Don't feel this is a perk for your own class only. That way you have to train up afresh each year. If you find an efficient pair, keep them as they move up through the school. They are worth their weight in gold. It is well worth spending time demonstrating how to do the basics properly, because you will only have to do so once. In a secondary school, your helpers will become sophisticated enough to pass on their skills to their eventual replacements.

Where to put your board display?

Position is important. Beg or fight for at least one large board in the front corridor near the Head's room. Visiting parents etc. can then see it whenever they pop in. How better to spend their inevitable waiting period than in inspecting your boards? Here they can see details about the next French play, the newspaper, the fashion show or the trip abroad. Especially useful as a recruiting aid for the latter are alluring photos of the most recent trip – comical (member of staff falling off donkey) or inviting (happy children leaning over the rail of the ferry watching France approach, or sunbathing on the beach). If your trip is a day-trip, you won't have time to take many photos yourself, so organise a competition for the 'best photo'. The children always have photos worth seeing (plus a few you would rather *not* see). On these boards you can also put up some of the material you have garnered for the final trip meeting for parents, such as posters of the area visited or to be visited (see Chapter 9) and, if nothing topical is going on, pictures of France in general. A display of Paris is always popular, as long as the irresistibly attractive Eiffel Tower is the main part of it.

Carried away with enthusiasm

I do not recommend you include *real money* in any of your displays. Before a day trip to Boulogne I once put up a display of francs, complete with the new coins, in the front hall (using sticky tape). We were taking parents with us that year, none of whom had been to France, and I thought it would be useful preparation for them. Older and wiser colleagues murmured about the wisdom of this course of action, but I assured them that the front hall was far too well-frequented for anyone to have time to take coins down. Well, of course, the inevitable happened, and the ten franc coins disappeared almost as soon as they went up. Nobody said 'I told you so', but I felt foolish. However, all was for the best, because the main suspect was soon apprehended, parading his haul to his friends. This worked out very well for me, as he was a paid-up member of the day trip about whom I had been having misgivings because of his serious light-fingered tendencies. Several colleagues had also suggested that he might be a problem.

What to do with the 'disaffected young'

However, I firmly believe that no-one should be barred from visiting a foreign country because of their past misdeeds, or 'reputation' for being a troublemaker. I never refuse to take anyone. But I do make it clear that I will take no-one who seriously misbehaves in the weeks before we go e.g. stealing or fighting or bullying. This is the time when they have to prove to me that they *can* behave as well as they assure me they *will* behave in France. In this way I often end up leaving behind the worst offenders. With this incident, I was able to bar the boy from the trip, to the great relief of all. Because so-called 'troublemakers' are on the whole extremely keen to go abroad, improved behaviour usually prevails in the weeks leading up to departure, and I am always glad to take them. Although they require discreet supervision, it seems to me that the disaffected young benefit more from the widened horizons of a visit to a foreign country than anyone else.

The attraction of the topical

When displaying items of interest about France, try and be topical whenever possible, even if you cannot find authentic materials. If you or the school can afford it, subscribe to something like 'Paris Match'. If not, persuade a French colleague to keep some old magazines or other for you, and reciprocate. Bring back a few from your visits. Then use pictures and print for your boards. If all else fails, cut out colourful pictures from English magazines and supply a caption in the foreign language. It is better than nothing. Opportunities like the 1989 celebrations and the opening of the Channel Tunnel have not presented themselves in recent years, but we always have the Tour de France, which can be popular with boys especially, not to mention the 1998 World Cup and Euro 2000 celebrations (tactful handling required here!). Do not miss out on current popular interest in *anything* that happens in the country of your second language. Even the sad accident of Princess Diana's death on the banks of the Seine was an opportunity. An event of such importance to us, taking place in a foreign country, somehow brought the two nations closer together. Many people were surprised to see television pictures of Parisians bringing flowers to the spot and mourning her as sincerely as we did, and a real connection was for a time forged between the two countries.

Intrigue the more advanced learner

Try and have a friend in the country whose language you teach. It is a great boon. Especially if you do not manage to go there as often as you would like. They can send you suitable items for display and, if they are a colleague, you can respond in the same way. This can be a particularly useful way of acquiring more sophisticated display material for older pupils e.g. 'A traditional moral homily': 'Statuts pour le Club des Fatigués de Naissance', or Dorothy Law Nolte's inspirational 'rules for the education of the young: Chaque enfant apprend par l'exemple'. I have seen older learners intrigued by that famous old poem 'Le Bon Gîte' by Paul Déroulède, or 'L'Amitié' by Sarah Biguet, all sent to me by a colleague in France. For some reason, because the work is on the wall and not in the textbook, and because they know it is authentically French, more advanced learners find it a challenge, and will struggle quite independently to decipher the mystery. I try not to interfere with them by offering help. For younger groups, we might have comical postcards or the menu for the week's school dinners at his school and countless other items. My colleague also organised penfriends for anyone who wanted one. He was invaluable.

Getting hold of authentic materials

This is all very well, you may be saying, but what if I don't have an obliging colleague at my disposal? How do *I* get hold of materials for display? When I was a new teacher and in the same position, I found there was only one way. You have to forage. Never make a visit to your foreign country without a second, totally empty, suitcase. While you are there, spend every waking moment filling it with:

(1) Top of the list: magazines. For pictures, cartoons, wonderful ads, topical items, horoscopes, lonely hearts, absolutely everything. Scrounge them from any household you visit.
(2) Tourist material, maps, pictures, general information. Can be found at the local 'Syndicat'.
(3) Publicity leaflets e.g. advertising wine (from shops).
(4) Supermarket posters (incredibly large and colourful in France).
(5) Store catalogues.
(6) A tricolore or two.
(7) Bus, train, metro tickets, timetables, etc.
(8) Holiday brochures. (Most intriguing are those advertising trips to Britain.)
(9) Superior pictorial maps of France. These look especially good with postcards you have collected on your travels arranged on all sides, ribbon or arrow pointing to the area.
(10) Basic food items for a first year shop.
(11) Almost anything else!

Developing your hawk eye

Do not despair if you never seem to get more than a quick dash on a day trip to forage. If you never get there at all, there are many sources of display material available to you over here. It may not be 'authentic' but it is effective.

(1) The French tourist office, Piccadilly.
(2) Any travel agent. Help yourself from the racks outside. Beautiful French holiday brochures with pictures of France to die for – especially the Eiffel Tower!
(3) French magazines on sale everywhere, particularly for their attractive and amusing ads, always interesting from a language point of view.
(4) English magazines: lots of intriguing advertisements for French goods. Plus publicity articles about the country.
(5) Cartoons. Replace the English caption with a translation.
(6) IT software.
(7) Articles spotted by the class in magazines at home (reward with a merit point).

Your room an Aladdin's cave of authentic materials

Of course, you will have taken pains to make your room as French as possible, with glossy pictorial maps (never Ordinance Survey!), posters, supermarket publicity spreads, signs and many other fruits of your foraging. Turn some of your bookshelves into 'the French shelves', where all can browse through travel brochures, catalogues, magazines etc. The dictionaries for class use might also be there, plus the very large picture books used for artwork (e.g. 'The first thousand words in French', Amery, Folio and Cartwright, Usborne). Above, have display shelves for French items the children bring in in order to receive a merit point (item returned later if required). Start off with a beautiful champagne bottle and it will quickly be followed by a large selection of wine and brandy bottles. I never ask from where they have been scavenged (in one school the rumour spread around that I was an alcoholic!), smoked glass cups, souvenirs, cosmetic boxes and bottles and a hundred things you would not imagine were made in France. In a corner, you might set up your first-year shop with all authentic packets and tins. It's a good idea to have all your materials stored in boxes from France, whether on view or in the cupboard, easy to pick up at any English supermarket (usually wine or apples). Children on the whole are consummate collectors, and may become more obsessed with the theme of display than you can cope with. Remember to rein them in when it comes to one souvenir item which you will quickly find you have in abundance. It will soon be filling up the display shelves to the exclusion of all else. Yes, you've guessed it, put your foot down – two models *only* of the dreaded Eiffel Tower!

As many computers as you can get into your classroom

Parents particularly like to see computer work on display. There are wonderful visuals which can look impressive on the wall in most of the IT language packages. Try and have access to a colour printer. If not, careful colouring in felt tip pen can be almost as good. Your computer buffs will probably have more ideas than you have. Whatever it is, it needs to be stuck carefully on coloured backing paper to make a frame, dark red or blue are ideal. You can also make impressive notices for Open Evening in the same way. Cover them in plastic and you can drag them out again and again for the same occasion. A similar treatment will produce elegant and long-lasting mini-tricolores coloured by pupils, which can deck your room in a riot of colour. If you take them down the day after and store them, they will last for years! Negotiate, plead, hassle or beg for as many computers as you can get into your classroom. You cannot have too many. Don't worry about your own skills. This is the special charm of teaching IT. You can rely on your class. Whatever *you* cannot do in this area, some of the children can.

Fear of the unfathomable and the unpredictable

Many years ago, when computers first came into schools, our staff had the traumatic experience of being given, by some wonderfully generous charity or other, a computer for each class. I knew nothing about them whatsoever. I would definitely rather have been asked to teach open-heart surgery. But worse was to come – these computers could not be left to moulder neglected in a corner or used by a few independent experts – we were timetabled to give one IT lesson a week to our own class! Which pleased the children enormously. Also the parents. They were all raring to go. As the person in charge of bringing my class into the twenty-first century, I was somewhat less enthusiastic. Each week we assembled in the new IT room, confronted by a great battery of computers, preparing to give our all. But unfortunately I am basically a non-technological sort of person (which was why I knew nothing about computers in the first place). I knew instinctively that computers were something like the internal combustion engine or modern central heating controls – unfathomable and totally unpredictable. However, there *was* hope. In order to enable us all (even me) to perform this miracle, all staff were sent on – yes, even in those days we had them – a course.

Teacher performing marvels

Every week we assembled at the local teachers' IT centre and were taught how to perform marvels on the computers there. To my surprise, it was quite easy. I took the precaution of writing notes, although we were not supposed to do so. Each week I would rush into school next day, eagerly clutching my notes, and looking forward to the looks of amazement on the faces of my class when I demonstrated the skill I had learned the night before, and the satisfaction we would all have as we produced wonderful work. Teachers at the centre had even copied pictures from our textbook onto a disc for us to use in all sorts of creative ways. Unfortunately it never turned out like that. Something seemed to happen when I sat at my own class computer which did not happen at the IT centre. (Or more often, vice versa!) Don't ask me what it was, but I could never reproduce the results I had achieved the night before. Not just occasionally, but consistently. If the children had not been a perpetual source of knowledge and support our progress would have been poor.

Angels rescued by Class 7, or divine intervention?

The year we started our first IT lessons one of our projects was to print out the French carol the whole school was singing at the Christmas carol service. Flushed with success from my lesson the night before, I suggested that we probably had the skills now to include a picture, just one, at the top. Clutching one I had completed with absolutely no difficulty at the teachers' centre, plus notes on how I did it, I was totally confident. What could go wrong? Lined up at our computers the class waited with bated breath for my instructions. Inserting and decorating with our own pictures had been a project close to our hearts from the start, and this was 'Sainte Nuit', therefore a very attractive Madonna and Child, surrounded by angels. We all felt it was a beautiful illustration, with heart-warming colouring implications. However, for one reason or another, the picture just would not come down, and there was nothing I could do about it, notes or no notes. (Lesson learnt: 'never promise the world in an IT lesson'.) I am not a religious person, but in view of the nature of the enterprise, I did call on God for help, and perhaps He did, because the children eventually worked it out and the school was able to enjoy an illuminated French carol sheet for the first time, angels and all.

Teacher as learner

The children's huge satisfaction with their success and the general atmosphere of celebration seemed to leave no room for my own personal feelings of 'teacher failure'. The initial idea that I might have been 'humiliated' by knowing less than my pupils, didn't seem to occur to anyone but myself, so I eventually gave it up. They had enjoyed helping me to success in exactly the same way I enjoyed helping them, and what could be better? This is when I learnt that teaching IT can be a sort of communal enterprise. In the average class, there is a great range of IT ability, from the complete beginner to (thank heaven) the expert. The teacher could be anywhere in between. The beauty of this democracy is that the teacher, no longer the leader, and the class, can all progress together.

Note to Chapter 7

1. Buzan, T. (1993) *The Mindmap Book*. London: BBC Books.

Chapter 8

Working independently – the French folder

Q Will they want to learn a foreign language?
Q What is the point?
Q Is there a case for the giving of French names?
Q How can you make the subject more personal?
A On the whole probably not, it is up to you to catch their interest
A Point out the practical advantages
A Yes, with appropriate groups
A Let them choose their own personal record in a permanent folder

Sun, sea and Sangria

All your efforts at display and information about the country have as their objective the bringing closer to the learner of its culture and everything about it. Your learners must feel that this is a real place, a desirable place, which is worth learning about. Unless you can achieve this, motivation will be affected. Some children will already have this interest, but never forget that for many of those that you teach, a foreign language may seem completely 'foreign' i.e. distant and unreal. If your school is in a suburb that is far from 'leafy', you will probably have this particular problem to wrestle with, not forgetting a certain amount of good old British working-class xenophobia. If you teach Spanish, you have an advantage. The children may have been to Spain, or have realistic expectations of going there one day. They know people who go there and are clear that it is a desirable place to be. They know all about sea, sun and Sangria. This being so, you may be able to persuade them that learning Spanish is a useful thing to do – but only slightly useful, because as someone will be sure to point out, 'everyone speaks English out there anyway'! On the other hand, if you teach French as I did, or one of the other European languages, your class will not hesitate to tell you that:

(1)   they have never been to France;
(2)   their parents have never been to France;
(3)   they don't know anyone who *has* been to France;
(4)   they never *will* go to France.

All of which is probably true, but does not help with motivation.

Respect their views

The children in some schools will be used to dragging along unwillingly behind the teacher, studying a subject they consider to be a complete waste of time. This is not a good learning situation, and must be altered. Only you can alter it. It is useful to start any beginners' lesson with an open discussion about the purpose of what we are doing. Open up the issue, listen to their genuine feelings and accept them. I usually begin with the question 'Why do you think we are going to learn French?' Although a few considerate souls will come up with the sort of positive answer they know teachers like to hear, the eventual consensus seems to be that we are learning it because it is on the curriculum. When they realise that you really *do* want to hear their honest views and will not be in the least put out by them, some will reveal that they regard the whole thing as a waste of time, and give their reasons for doing so. Do not make judgements, start from where they are. This whole process reminds me of research I read about years ago, asking 15-year-olds whether they thought learning a language was:

(1)   useful and interesting;
(2)   useful but boring;
(3)   useless and boring.

Useless and boring?

I was shocked to see the results, particularly how many came into Category 3, but like to think things have improved along the way. I am sure they have.[1] However, this information emphasised for me the importance of keeping in touch with learners' real, as opposed to 'polite' views. Teachers can sometimes be out of touch with the social environment of their particular learners, and it is easy to make assumptions about the view of the wider world a child brings to school from home. As a grammar school girl, I had no problems with motivation. I fully expected to visit France, was eager to do an exchange at the earliest opportunity, and could easily visualise working there at some future stage in my life. If you have a similar background, remember that many of your students do not, and you are going to have to compensate for that. When I later came to teach in a 'non-leafy' school, I had to compensate single-handed, quite a tall order. How is it to be done?

Forget Napoleon

When all have aired their views and had those views accepted, move on to suggest some of the advantages to them that speaking a European language could bring. To do this you must discuss the completely new situation we are in since ties with Europe became closer, and the fact that they can only grow closer in the future. I usually mention:

(1)   France is our nearest neighbour after Ireland (a little geography?).

(2) Some of the more positive historical connections (the Second World War, *not* Napoleon?).
(3) Advantages of being part of Europe (*not* 'Golden Delicious'?).
(4) Importance of being able to work in Europe in the future (speaking only English will not do).
(5) Career prospects in this country for anyone able to speak a European language (show a few advertisements from that day's paper?).
(6) Learning one language makes it easier to learn another (for the sangria-philes).

Don't go OTT

You may be surprised how little your class knows about the European Community, and why we are in it. Enlighten them. There is lots of good material to be found in most textbooks. Introduce them to the larger world in which they are going to live, comprising the whole of Europe and its opportunities. Mention how likely it is that, for workers in England, out of two identically qualified applicants for the same job, the one with the foreign language will get it. Mention that modern language graduates have lower unemployment rates than any others, including Maths and Physics.[2] Work to counter the xenophobia they may encounter in the media or at home. But don't work too hard. Keep cool. If you seem to them to be too enthusiastic, what you say will be discounted. Let them hear the calm information-giver, rather than the over-the-top Francophile.

Widening their world

Having pointed out ways in which a foreign language might be relevant to their future, the next step is to introduce them to the culture they will be getting to know as they learn. It is impossible to learn a language without experiencing the identity of the country in which it is spoken, and this is one of the most educational aspects of the whole process. Learners are not just learning a new language, they are entering into a new world. In this new world live others who do not see the world in quite the same way as they themselves do. They are different. They have different customs and different ideas. And yet they turn out, on closer acquaintance, to be so very like ourselves. Despite difference, the similarities are greater. Learning to understand and empathise with fellow human beings in this way is a powerful area of personal growth.

'Why do they drive on the wrong side of the road, Miss?'

You will see your younger learners (and perhaps some of the older ones!) struggle with this idea for a while. There are looks of disbelief, e.g.: 'in France you start in Class 6 and work up to Class 1') or even disgust, e.g.: 'In France you eat everything off the same plate!', but it is mainly an internal struggle. It may surface occasionally with a deeply-felt appeal such as: 'But why do they say 'dress blue' instead of 'blue dress', Miss?' or 'Why don't they do it like us?' These are difficult questions to answer briefly, involving as they do centuries of complicated and often forgotten historical development, and I usually answer 'Why don't we do it their way?' But I confess that this is more for my own satisfaction than to answer the question, which it certainly does not … It is natural for any culture to assume that theirs is the 'proper' way of doing things, and you can only point this out, provided your audience has reached a stage of maturity where it can accept the idea. Do not succumb to the irresistible urge to run through the entire history of the two countries, starting with the Greeks and Romans. It may be very satisfying and informative to *you*, but is not the answer they are looking for. Basically, you have a choice between curt certainty ('all countries do these things differently'), or whatever more (or less) thorough explanation of the offending custom seems appropriate for those particular listeners at that particular time. (Go easy on the Latin!)

No, no, Ninette!

From this point on you have only one major weapon in your armoury. You must bring the country you want them to know into their lives using whatever means you can. Disseminating information through display for the whole school, class or parents is an important element, but you can start at the other end of the scale, as you might say, by giving very young learners – yes, this may surprise you – a French name. This always seemed to me to be a terribly old-fashioned thing to do, and something I would never stoop to. I know adults who have never recovered from the embarrassment of their French name at school. I myself loathed mine, and suffered agonies of shame when forced to reveal it. I can hardly bring myself to mention it now. But on reflection, I realised that I was given the wrong name at the wrong developmental stage. I began learning French at the age of eleven. We were quite a sophisticated group of 11-year-olds too. It seemed an unwarrantable condescension. The worst thing was that we were allocated names willy-nilly and given no choice. I swore that name-giving would never be a part of my repertoire if I ever became a teacher of languages (nothing could be less likely, of course).

Younger classes – a golden opportunity

Later in my career I moved from comprehensive to middle school and began to teach children starting at a very young age nine. This was a whole different ball game. These learners are very special. They are totally open, totally enthusiastic, and totally eager to please. They love you and they want you to love them. They are one big opportunity for the language teacher. Giving them a new, exotic name seemed at once to be appropriate. It was a sort of response to their need for intimacy and individual attention. My instinct was correct, they enjoyed it very much, choosing the new name with lots of thought and teaching it to family at home and to all their friends. (I would quite like to choose a new name myself from time to time).

They were very disappointed if teacher forgot it, as teacher unfortunately did from time to time. Because they took it so seriously it was a boost to their self-esteem. Only you can tell if your modern class will value such a time-honoured procedure, but it can be very rewarding, and makes the language more relevant to the learner in the most concrete of ways (e.g. 'The President of France has the same name as me!')

A personal stake in the new language

We made the introduction of names an important and painstaking ritual. It took place during relaxation breaks when illustration and copying of new material would be quietly pursued. I made two large cards, one for girls and one for boys, with a comprehensive list of the most acceptable and familiar French names I could muster. (Ninette did not feature.) Our very first relaxation work was the inscribing and felt-tip colouring of pupil names, in the biggest possible letters, on the top half of the document wallet supplied for this age group instead of exercise books. The aim of this manoeuvre was not exactly educational, but very worthwhile – it was to allow teacher to walk round the room learning everyone's name at a glance. (You can guess what the bottom half was left empty for …) As each child finished this piece of work – in satisfactorily bright colours – they were allowed the great privilege of coming up to my desk to consult 'the name card'. We took this very seriously. I had to read out the pronunciation of favoured names to each individual, so that they did not choose on the basis of English pronunciation e.g. Catherine, Angelique, Jean, Louis. When they had made their choice, some taking longer than others, some completely unable to decide and being left until another day, I wrote the name on a piece of paper for them to take back to their seats and copy onto their folder, in writing identically large and colourful to the English name. I could see them all easily walking round the class. From there on in I addressed them by the new name whenever possible and they glowed with pride. Those without French names looked on enviously. If anyone seemed less than enthusiastic I gave them a second chance to choose, but very few did. I could not help wondering if I would have been able to enjoy a name that I had chosen myself? Perhaps. (In case you are wondering, it was 'Ninette'!)

Using the contents of your suitcase

The folder is more than a memory aid for the teacher, nor is it something special for young beginners only. A class of any age might like to make one, and their folder can accompany them through the school, if carefully looked after. Parents like to look at them on parents' evening. It is to be the learner's own collection of material to do with France – pictures, artwork, authentic materials, adverts, tourist information, anything they choose. (Now you know what the suitcase was for!). Try to have a brightly coloured document wallet for each child as this will appeal more to their imagination. If your school cannot run to it, coloured sugar paper folded over will do. By coloured I do not mean the drab and dreary greys and beiges that school sugar paper seems often to come in. Why this should be so I have no idea (is it cheaper?), but bring what influence, if any, you have to bear on the person who does the ordering. These colours and quality of paper are almost impossible to make look attractive, stick on it, or colour it as you may. Insist on the slightly better shades which can be had, or even better quality paper or card. Disintegrating s.p. covers will have to be replaced from time to time, but this can be an opportunity to try something new, and a particularly favourite cover picture can always be re-stuck. Make sure the folder is large enough to hold A4 sheets, that is, slightly bigger, but not too big. I once allowed some boys to make themselves giant folders but they were nothing but trouble (the folders, not the boys). They flapped about and things fell out all over the place. Also they were more difficult to store, not fitting on shelves or in most drawers.

Appealing to their personal interests

When everyone has made or acquired a folder, with the exception of young beginners, who already have names inscribed on theirs, have the class select and stick on the cover an eye-catching picture of France. You will find plenty of these in the tourist brochures you have procured around the town. Whilst they are browsing through these publications they are already picking up a little of the feel of the country. Speaking of which, never let anyone stick anything onto anything *until you have checked it*. Someone will always find a more creative way of cutting out the ladies of the Folies Bergères who often feature in tourist brochures. Asian parents can be easily offended and care must be taken in this area e.g. the lingerie section of home catalogues. Then they are free to include whatever they like, provided it has been passed by you, with the proviso that at least half must be their own work. There are many sources of ideas for items which involve France and appeal to the learner's personal interests. Some of them can simply be fun. On your display shelf or about the room, you will have several of the large picture books aimed at young children, which have an enduring appeal to all ages, e.g. '*I Can Read French*' by Penrose Colyer (Peter Lowe Publishers), '*The First Thousand Words in French*' by Amery, Folio and Cartwright (Usborne), and '*Discovering French with Walt Disney*' (Chambers Harrap). For younger learners HarperCollins have brought out a delightful '*First 100 Words in French and English*' with a tab to pull revealing each language in turn. The top favourite with everybody is the book with the duck!

No artwork without French caption

Learners of all ages seem to find these pictures more appealing than any text-book, and enjoy copying one or two favourites for their folder, with French caption. No artwork of any sort goes in without a French caption of course. If they are desperate to include something which has no caption, do one for them.

Older pupils can find one themselves. Old textbooks can be useful also. Many of them have simple cartoons which are ideal. The Mary Glasgow *'French for the National Curriculum'* series is a wonderful resource for folder items, with its beautiful graphics and brief accompanying information in the ML. Ideal for reproduction and interesting too (especially Book F, *'Vaste Monde'*). Unfortunately publication was discontinued in 1999, but if you can get hold of a set second-hand, snap it up. Should the owner be allowed to copy information in English about France for his folder, you may be wondering. That is entirely up to you. I would make an exception for this, provided it was something very special for the particular learner, and as long as s/he had much that was in French as well. After all, this is independent learning, and s/he has shown initiative in finding the material. It's usually something like 'Incredible Facts about France' culled from who knows where …?

Their own personal treasure chest

Try and find out what the interests of each pupil are and help them to express them, be it sport, animals, computer games or ballroom dancing. There is literally no end to the topics which can be represented in the folder, with French caption, from cut-outs from a French clothes catalogue to an article about a footballer from a magazine, from a list of road signs to a favourite gourmet recipe. The signs of the zodiac, a family tree, pictures of pets at home or zoo animals, labelled in French or a letter from a French penfriend (even better, a whole correspondence). Give those who like puzzles a grid on which to make a wordsearch or crossword and have a plastic map of France for younger pupils (and some older ones) to draw round. Then they can find places they have heard of to label – easier since the World Cup '98! The map stencil is very popular with younger children, as an easy means to produce a good quality result. Even more popular with older learners, particularly for wall display as well as folder, is a bizarre miracle of cutting and sticking – the large coloured picture cut out of a magazine, stuck on A4 and then labelled in French e.g. a body-builder with body parts labelled (discreetly of course). You can have a whole corridor board full of them and vote for the best. The rest of the school will be very interested. There is something strangely comical about these pictures. They have nothing in common with a drawing and can be very creative. But beware of the boy or girl who wants to fill the entire folder with such pictures, or perhaps computer work, if that is his or her bent. Insist on having a range of items in each folder, in order to build up a picture of the country. Encourage them to make a collage of French realia, or to bring in pictures and articles about France from home, not necessarily for their own use only, rewarding with a merit point. Never despise merit points …

Watch out for the unruly budgie

When the children actually visit the country they will come back with a rich harvest of authentic items, and if of a literary bent, could write an interesting account of their day-trip or visit to include in their folder. If they stay at home, they can always rely on the teacher's suitcase! Remind them that their folders will be on show to parents and other visitors at times, and can be taken home at the end of the year if they wish. (Those with unruly budgies will be allowed to leave theirs at school until next term.) They are usually quite interested in taking them home and you will be surprised at the pride that is taken in the finished object. At the end of one year, I gave the folder of an absent Year 8 pupil to a friend of his to take home for him, as they were not coming back to school the following year. Somewhere between homes it went astray. I was pleased to receive more than one enquiry about the lost folder from its owner, showing real concern.

Resign yourself to the inevitable

Because effort is such a large element in the success of this project, I like to award a small prize for the best folders in each class at the end of the year. In some classes it will be one only, in others three or four. When I say 'small prize' I really mean 'small' – perhaps something like a Mars bar! The prize itself is of no importance, it's the honour of being the best that counts. This is the only kind of prize I ever award, because it is above all a reward for hard work, which means that it is open to all. Before I finish, there is one very important item I forgot to mention, one which you cannot afford to be without. It is a stencil of the Eiffel Tower. This is essential. It is for those who cannot draw. Those who have not experienced twenty badly drawn Eiffel Towers will have no idea how badly drawn an Eiffel Tower can be. Fortunately most of the class will be able to copy their own from a picture. Those who cannot, try to interest in something else, something less challenging, like a bateau-mouche or the front view of Notre Dame, or even Sacre Coeur! You will probably not succeed. Nothing else captures their imagination in the same way, I am afraid to say. So give up, and have your stencil at the ready, because you can be sure of one thing – every folder will have one.

Notes to Chapter 8

1. Lee, J., Buckland, D. and Shaw, G. (1998) *The Invisible Child*. London: CILT.
2. Footitt, H. (2000) Losing our tongues just when we need them. *Guardian Higher Education*, 1st February 2000, 3H.

LE GOLFE

JOIE IMMENSE

à 8 Barford Avenue au mois de février.
Darren Stokes est rentré à la maison après
trois mois de service militaire au Golfe.
Darren est le frère de Nicola Stokes (7^{10}).
Pendant six mois, les soldats alliés de
l'Europe et de l'Amérique se sont battus
avec le dictateur Saddam Hussein. Final-
ment, la victoire - il a été chassé de Kuwait.
Autres soldats de la région étaient Bobby
Giles, frère de Paul Giles 6^{13}, Deborah Burr
cousine de Jonathan Fox (7^{10}) et l'oncle de
Wayne (7^9) Anthony (7^6) et David (6^{12})
Marlow.

Toutes les familles de Silver Jubilee, élèves
et professeurs, souhaitent le bienvenue à
nos soldats courageux!

—Vous avez déjà fait du ski nautique?   —Non, je n'ai jamais fait de ski nautique.

Vacances 1991: Monsieur Hutchings à Malibu

Chapter 9

Open evenings

Q What are they for?
Q How far to go?
Q What are parents/prospective parents looking for?
Q Should I talk to the parents or wait for them to talk to me?
A Open evenings are a PR exercise
A Avoid panic by preparing well in advance and having pupil help
A A snapshot of what takes place in your classroom. Display all your equipment, organise a variety of self-generating activities, and look forward to *showing off*!
A Choose browsing parents with care

Teacher and sales executive

Preparing for an Open Evening can be stressful. Whether for prospective parents, existing parents, or both, it is an advertisement for the school. The head of your school knows how vital this is and will be relying on you to create a good impression. Schools have become products on an open market and have to be sold, not a concept which has instant appeal to most teachers, who prefer to concentrate on what they have always seen as their job – the education of young people. But once you have become accustomed to the idea, look on the bright side. It is a great opportunity to show-off!

Avoid live elephants

Because the Headteacher will want all the rooms to be open, you will generally be responsible for the preparation of your own personal area, and the manning, or womaning, of it alone, throughout the evening, or perhaps day. You will be very much aware that the impression your area creates will be entirely up to you (the Robinson Crusoe effect), and wonder how to achieve a suitably dynamic and serious, yet inviting effect. You may feel that extraordinary measures are called for.

They are not. It is important to avoid doing too much. Reduce stress by ignoring totally the example of some other departments. Do not stroll round earlier in the week and look at what they are doing. Especially avoid the Science department, who will have converted their labs into an inferno of scientific activity, splitting the atom in Room 1, and presenting the life cycle of the elephant in Room 2 (with real elephants). Nor should you compete with Art. You do not have at your disposal a kiln, five hundred clay models of a foot, five hundred budding Picassos or one hundred self portraits by Year 9. Not to mention the array of fast-food boxes.

Quasimodo on the ramparts (with bells)?

You do not have their resources (with the possible exception of models of the E.T.), nor storage areas, and your room will be quite 'other'. Don't be tempted to aim at a microcosm of France or wherever, with pavement cafe, people in striped jerseys and waiters on roller blades. Or real imported Italians chatting under a model of the leaning Tower of Pisa. Colleagues I have known who indulged in this kind of thing ended up nervous wrecks. (I speak as the person who thought the entire modern languages department doing the can-can three nights running on the school concert was *a good idea*.) Balance the effect of any such project with the time/energy cost to you. How will teaching time be affected? After all, Open Evenings have little educational pay-off for the pupil. Instead, ask yourself what the visitors are probably hoping to see? What do you yourself want to see when you visit as a parent? When I first asked myself that question I decided that what I really wanted was something like this: a snapshot of what happens on a day to day basis for learners in that room (in other words, what my child would actually be *doing*), plus information about the teaching methods and resources used.

Creating an atmosphere of panic

With a similar scenario as your aim these regular public relations exercises need not entail an enormous amount of work, provided you have them in mind throughout the year and – this is vital – hoard your materials. Very little preparatory running around in circles is needed. Create an Open Day box in which you deposit likely material the whole year round. This will go a long way to avoiding an attack of teacher 'pre-traumatic stress syndrome', that is, you rushing around like a demented ferret the whole week before. By falling into this trap, you are in danger not only of neglecting your teaching, but of creating an atmosphere of mad panic on the evening, instead of the relaxed enthusiasm you are aiming at. It is really just a matter of getting everything out on display and then putting it all away again. By 'everything' I mean *all* your teaching resources, because parents and prospective parents will be interested in more than just exercise books and textbooks. Nowadays, your target group is *prospective* parents. In these days of competition and league tables, parents shop around as never before, and your headteacher will be relying on you (and the rest of the staff) to lure in parents who were thinking of sending their child elsewhere. On Open Evening you have to be not only a teaching but a marketing expert. When the public come into your domain, think 'estate agent'!

Soothe the savage breast

I find the key to a successful Open Evening is a cheerful, Gallic (or other) atmosphere. The best way to achieve this is to play background music. A room with music is a room where people linger. The teacher of French has an inestimable advantage here – French music is particularly appealing to British audiences and always has been. (Notice recent television advertisements using Trenet's 'Boum!') For Italian there is opera, popular as never before through football, and Spain has flamenco. But choose carefully. I'm afraid Edith Piaf will *not* do. Choose traditional accordion, or artists popular over here, like Trenet or Chevalier – something which parents will recognise as quintessentially French. In other words, not favourites of your own, which you have learnt to love over the years (Jacques Brel?) These will probably not be sufficiently accessible to the first-time listener.

Parents love equipment

Your walls will probably be ready for an open day at any time, with colourful displays by the children (including computer work), holiday brochures and a display of French realia all giving a flavour of the place (see Chapter 7). These make the room bright and welcoming and give the visitors something to look at. Next, set up for each year group, a table or other area, under a large sign indicating which year, and place upon it a sample exercise book, a textbook, flashcards, worksheets (completed), a few folders, conversation cards, computer work and any other materials used by the children in that year. Do not forget the important audio-tapes. With the tapes put transcripts and head-sets so that parents can listen if they would like to. Many parents have remnants of 'O' level languages which can be resuscitated, or more current holiday language learning which they would enjoy dusting down. At the very least, the presence of audio material tells them something about the focus of the teaching methods employed. Looking around, the parents can examine exactly what their own children are doing, or will be doing, in lessons. Do not just heap things up here and there leaving visitors to work out what they are. Let your classes make large card labels for everything, and next to each textbook place the teacher's book, which will hopefully explain all (!). Have every piece of equipment you possess on show (computers, OHP, TV, video cassettes, tape recorders, head-sets etc.), because parents love equipment. You, of course, will spend the evening hovering, available but not pushy, waiting to answer any questions.

Why some photos of staff are less suitable than others

To take the subject beyond the classroom, display entertaining photos from the latest French trip, if they are not already on display in a more strategic position, like the front hall. Not only are these usually quite humorous, but they help with recruitment for next year's trip. They should not be *too* entertaining however. Parents do not always appreciate the 'joie de vivre' which can accompany these occasions. Photos of the French play or fashion show, and a few copies of your school 'Journal' should also be there, but do not be disappointed if most visitors ignore the 'Journal', once realising it is in French. Do not despair however, with luck you may be able to bully a more amenable visitor into appreciation of how accessible it really is to the non-French speaker.

Let there be fun

Have a table with children playing games, just as they do in class. This is more interesting for the parents than poring over their child's work, and they will probably be impressed by the players' natural use of French. But don't have *too many* tables or children. Too many children is never a good idea. More than six will become a supervision item and a distraction, when all your energies should be going into relating with parents and other visitors. This is a quick and easy activity to organise and can be done as late as the day before. Helpers will be keen and if they are not, bring out the merit points. But don't forget to get parents' consent and check on how they are going to get home. Parents will not always be coming to the evening, or may not be able to stay until the end. You may end up having to take them yourself. I have never found it difficult to recruit for open evenings, but if it is, merit points should do the trick.

Catch them young – print-outs for toddlers

You could add to this group a couple of computer literati, showing off with language games etc. Make these the most skilled and confident you have, who never get into trouble on the computer or need to call for your help. You have no time to show off your own IT proficiency. (I am not suggesting, of course, that any embarrassment might result. Of course not. The problem obviously is that you would be distracted from the task in hand!). They might also be persuaded to cater for small visitors by offering them a choice of pictures with French caption, perhaps using 'Pendown'. They can be printed out for the children to take home with them. (Vet them all!) I say 'persuaded' because I have found pupils who are computer buffs to be rather independent-minded, with very definite ideas about what they want to do. Frequently not coinciding with what *you* want them to do. They are imaginative souls and have resources on the machine which you know nothing of. They will probably find your requirements insufficiently challenging, in which case you may have to resort to bribery. Print-outs for small children are worth doing, because when these pictures appear around the school, clutched in tiny hands, more visitors will be attracted.

Better than a gin and tonic

It came as a surprise to me, but answering questions on Open Evening about what you do day after day, can actually be rather *enjoyable*. Here you have an audience which tends to be less informed and less critical than the people you usually talk to about the detail of your work – not friends and family, but head of department, headteacher, colleagues, language advisors and such. This audience tends to fall somewhere between the two groups in terms of how interested and how appreciative it will be. (Only very occasionally will you have open criticism to cope with. Should this happen, listen pleasantly and excuse yourself. Do not be drawn into argument). You find yourself looking forward to the opportunity to explain exactly what you are trying to do, to share your enthusiasm, and to hear feedback from the other side of the learning machine, home. More than this, you hope to hear about learners who are enjoying their lessons and say so at home. Particularly gratifying is when parents remark on their surprise that their son or daughter actually 'likes French', because they themselves 'could never do it' A righteous glow may very well follow these comments, better than a gin and tonic. We are all human, and there is no doubt that such favourable comments are gratefully received.

The teacher nobody wanted

But sometimes you will find that people pass through your inviting room without noticing you. No-one seems to want to ask you any questions. They may be lingering well. They are interested in the materials on view and gaze at them in awe and wonder. They pick up this and that and examine it minutely. They walk round looking intently at the wall displays. They are the perfect visitors. But they avoid your eye. Then, joy of joys, one father approaches you. Your heart leaps. He tells you that you have made Matthew's verrucas worse by making him wear shoes instead of trainers. That is all. He has no interest of any kind in Matthew's progress in French. You are disappointed, you are hurt. What is going on? Can everything be totally self-explanatory? Are you redundant? This is bad for morale (yours), makes you wonder why they are not more curious, and worst of all, means you have nothing whatsoever to do.

Parents with school phobia

If this happens to you, you need to ask yourself exactly what impression you are making on the parents as they wander through. You are waiting for them to make contact with you. You are eager to convey to them the delights of language learning that await their offspring. But it is not enough just to be there. Are you sure you are hovering properly? The quality of your hovering dictates the number of questions you will have. There is an art to it. Do make sure that you hover enough. It is vital. Parents can often be overwhelmed by memories of their own childhood when they enter a school, and become again 'as little children'. Bear in mind that the most unlikely people – Chief Superintendents of Police, High Court judges and even members of the SAS, once went to school. Some of them were even quite naughty when they did so. Because old conditioning dies hard, they may be a little bit afraid of you. The poor things would like to ask questions but dare not approach you if they think there is the slightest chance that you may be 'busy'. That is: chatting to a colleague, eating a biscuit, looking at something (anything), drinking tea, or simply *not looking at them.*

Rules for the Art of Hovering
(1) Look alert and approachable.
(2) Do not chat.
(3) Do not look at anything.
(4) Do not stand about looking as if you are at a loose end.
(5) Observe everyone in the room all the time.
(6) Observe anyone looking even vaguely in your direction, and try to catch their eye.
(7) Do not sit down and read, or worse still, mark anything. This will be interpreted as being 'busy'.
(8) Do not sit down at all. This will also be interpreted as being 'busy'. (Especially do not sit down and drink coffee. If you can't get through the evening without refreshment – and this is very likely – drink standing up!)
(9) Do not join the children who are playing games or doing other activities in your room. (This is the hardest rule of all).
(10) Do not stare too intently at the parents. They may find it unnerving.
(11) You may find some of these rules contradictory.

The lion and his prey
When the parents are lingering and you are hovering, you have something in common with the lion stalking his prey. Your aim is to impress upon your visitors the excellence of your department and everything about it. You have tried to make this obvious by the quality of your display. At the same time you can't help feeling that many people passing through see only a pleasant and encouraging room. You would like to talk to them, answer their questions, if they have any, and generally make contact. You would like to pounce. (There are schools where you will have no such difficulty – keen parents will insist on questioning you about all aspects of work. No hovering will be required – *they* will pounce on *you*, and you are the prey.) But more often, you will have to consider your position on that most controversial of questions – 'to pounce or not to pounce'?

To pounce or not to pounce?

You are by nature either a 'lurker' or a 'pouncer'. Should you be sharing a room with a colleague who does not share your approach, look out for problems. The 'pouncer' will be determined to leap upon all who enter the lair, and give them a complete rundown of the aims and objectives of your department including an in-depth sprint through the National Curriculum. You will be seen as something of a shirker if you fail to do the same. The 'lurker' on the other hand will have decided to give visitors peace and quiet in which to browse, marvel and make their own discoveries. He or she will conceal with difficulty a desire to push the 'pouncer' into a cupboard. This is a matter of individual temperament, which cannot be helped, so if you are new to the school, find out if there is a department policy. And if there is no general rule, you may have to wrestle with your natural inclinations and co-exist happily, each doing your own thing. On the other hand, you may drive each other mad.

Standing about looking as if you are at a loose end

But few have the luxury of two members of staff in one area. So you are alone and have opted to lurk. Beware of the following situation. No-one has spoken to you for an hour. You are lonely and depressed. You are uncomfortably aware that you have succumbed to 'standing about looking as if you are at a loose end'. You survey the room in desperation and decide to pounce after all. You spot someone picking something up and examining it intently, or someone spending a very long time in one area. Surely here at last is someone who might like to talk about teaching methods or exam boards, homework policy or use of IT in the department, visits abroad or drama etc. or even the progress of one of your pupils, which is much more fun. But pause for a moment. Imagine yourself on a shopping trip. You are in 'ladieswear' or 'menswear', carefully working your way through rails of suits for your brother's wedding, deep in thought. You have a difficult decision to make. How to strike the right note – celebratory yet not too flamboyant? You are going to need time. How do you feel when the sales assistant interrupts you with offers of help? If on the other hand you have opted to pounce, don't forget the parents who 'just want to look' or who may be intimidated by your little lecture. If 'customers' begin to rush out of the room in panic, thus missing out on what could have been a positive experience of your subject, you may have gone too far.

Champagne all round?

Try to have something for everybody in your room. (Glasses of wine may be frowned on!) The number of parents attracted to each room will be generally regarded by headteacher and other staff as a sign of teacher success. The fact that it is a matter of public relations rather than quality teaching is beside the point. Good PR is not the same as good teaching and you will notice that some of the best teachers are incapable of putting on a 'good parents' evening'. Unfortunately league tables have rendered public relations at least as important as good teaching in our schools today. Your headmaster or mistress will reward those who sell their subject successfully (think washing powder!)

The assertiveness of Attila the Hun

Finally, if this is an evening for people considering whether to send their children to your school or not in the future, do not forget the most important item in the room, the item which will be the centre of the more discerning visitors' attention and which has to be the most attractive and inviting of all. Yes, of course – you. But do not make the mistake of trying to charm the 'customers'. Be nice, but not too nice. You do not want them to mistake you for a pushover. Some parents are looking above all for a teacher capable of coping with 'their Gary' (because they can't). Not to mention the ones looking for someone able to cope with other peoples' 'Garys'! You have the difficult task of appearing amiable, caring and entertaining, whilst at the same time hinting at the assertiveness of Attila the Hun and the iron discipline of Stalin. It is up to you exactly how you achieve this. Your real personality will probably shine through anyway.

Chapter 10

School visits – the day trip to France

Q Is it an easy option?
Q How can stress be reduced?
Q Why do they go?
Q Is it possible to go shopping in Boulogne in a party of 70?
Q What makes a pleasant and stress-free journey?
Q Worksheets – to be or not to be?
Q Can you prevent smuggling?
Q Are parents' meetings worth it?
Q Passports – an unavoidable pain?
Q All-school involvement – what for?
A It's arduous, but a vital way of motivating the majority
A Have good support, prepare well and be optimistic
A Because you have used the lure of a 'trip' as a means of exposing them to a different culture
A No. Use small groups and lots of staff 'being around'
A A 'day tripper's essential kit' and lots of rules
A Avoid them if you can get away with it
A Make a firm contract with all before you set out
A Parents are part of the all-school involvement
A Yes, so leave lots of time to sort them out
A So that next year you take even *more* children to France

The school trip: why?

What can be said about school trips abroad? The day excursion to Boulogne is a very different animal from the longer exchange visit (about which more later), but they are both worthwhile in their different ways. They are an essential part of the language learning experience. They make a reality out of what was a fiction; they foster international relations; they can transform a no-hoper into an enthusiast; they teach social skills like nothing else, especially if the trip involves living in a foreign family; they broaden horizons, even in one day; they can in some cases, though not all, modify British chauvinism; they encourage unlikely children to make an exchange visit later; they create a new relationship between teacher and taught; and they are the accompanying teachers' nightmare!

'Club Med' or 'Bridge on the River Kwai'?

Teachers embarking on trips abroad with children seem to be the envy of all. Colleagues, parents, children and the public at large, all believe that they are off on a carefree holiday free of charge. But this is not at all the case, as anyone who has actually tried it will tell you. I have chosen to start with the one day excursion, because it seems to me to be the most stressful type of visit, including the residential, perhaps because of the large numbers usually involved, reduced personal contact between staff and pupils, and the wider variety of child travelling. There are hidden stresses involved in this enterprise. What are they and what can be done to alleviate them?

(1) You and your colleagues are in 'loco parentis' for a large group of children, some of whom you hardly know, none of whom you know half as well as their actual parents.
(2) You are going to be travelling 'en masse', which means that any breakdown, strike or other hold-up will have more serious implications.
(3) Your responsibility for the safety of the party is total. You know that if a child in your care falls off a mountain, *you* will be to blame.
(4) All the things which go wrong on a normal family holiday will go wrong. Only to more people.

Taking up a relaxed attitude, or 'how's your swimming'?

These are some of the hidden stresses which you will gradually become aware of. Nothing will be further from your mind when you set off on your first trip. You see it as a wonderful opportunity to enjoy yourself abroad with the children. You are looking forward to a relaxing holiday. Until you begin your first journey, waving goodbye to the white cliffs of Dover, leaning over the rail with the excited children. One rather exuberant boy is pretending to push another overboard. Suddenly, you find yourself wondering what you would have done if the pretend push had become a reality. Would you have jumped in after him? Would you have taken your coat off first? Are you brave enough? Would you have been able to find him in all that churning water? Would you have been able to save his life if you did? Exactly how good is your swimming? Would you have run to summon a member of the crew? Would you have looked for a lifebelt to throw in first? Where would the child have been by that time? How long does it take one of these speeding vessels to leave behind someone in the water? You begin to feel a little anxious. Later, you wonder what you would have said to the Head on your return, and what he would have said to the parents …

The end of innocence

You realise suddenly that you are not going to be able to relax quite as you had anticipated. It occurs to you that you are not, in fact, in the 'position of a parent'.

Firstly, because you are responsible not just to yourself, but to the school and parents for the safety of all your party. That party may have a teacher/pupil ratio of anything, but it will certainly be greater than that of an average family outing. And secondly, because the behaviour of unattended children in groups is an entirely different thing from that of those travelling with their family. It tends to be more lively and unpredictable, and more open to peer pressure. Two or three hours into the journey you begin to feel the responsibility. If you are the carefree type, it may take longer. When this happens, you decide to step up your supervision and take to wandering round the boat a lot with a colleague. On arrival, you wander round the town in the same way, keeping an unobtrusive eye on your pupils. You sort out a few problems. Returning home, you sigh with relief on landing at Dover with all safe and well and nobody left behind. At school you hand them over to the happy parents and go home to sleep the sleep of the dead. You decide not to do it again. Was it worth it for just one day? The preparations were out of all proportion to the time spent abroad. Such a long day too. Everyone is exhausted. Definitely not. Never again. After a week or two, you begin to plan the next one.

Teacher–pupil bonding, or the child who was nearly run over

So why do teachers persist in taking their pupils abroad, particularly for just one day, if it is such a stressful experience? You will have heard a lot about language teaching strategies recently. Well, going abroad is the most vital one of all. If you can't bring the foreign country into the classroom, you can bring the classroom into the foreign country! And not just for those in the party. The intrepid travellers will tell tales to all their friends on their return. You will find yourself bonding in a new way with your pupils, both those who went on the trip and those who did not. And there will be fascinating feedback to you, as each class tells you what other people in other classes *really* did in Boulogne. You will hear all about the souvenirs that were brought back and what Dad thought of his Eiffel Tower; how Rachel got locked in the toilets on the boat, and how Nasreen 'didn't know that cars drive on the wrong side of the road over there and was nearly run over, 'just like you said, Miss!' Most of all there will be requests to go next year. From people who went and from people who didn't go. Somehow you will find yourself looking back fondly on the whole day. All the little successes and challenges and all the failures will be part of something bigger, something happy and fulfilling. In some strange way, both staff and children will feel that they have been tested and not found wanting. It's a good feeling. You will start making a list of plans for next year.

With a song in your heart

A school trip abroad is a bit like childbirth – when it's all over, you forget the pain. From the moment you get back, almost immediately, you will have forgotten what were your main areas of worry. But don't let that prevent you from addressing stress reduction techniques for next year. Who are these teachers who travel happily abroad with children year after year? What is their secret? Obviously someone has to do it, but why do some actually enjoy themselves and make lifelong friends in foreign places, whilst others loathe and avoid the whole experience? Is it just temperament, or practical survival techniques? If you are a 'worrier', are you bound to fail in this area? Not at all. We all know that 'worriers' can be invaluable colleagues. (They are the people who come into their own in an emergency – they have just what you need in their bag!) So how do teachers, including 'worriers', who regularly enjoy accompanying school journeys, do it? By developing techniques, both practical and psychological, which work for them to relieve anxiety. Some of these are:

(1) First priority: the selection of reliable colleagues. Supervision, particularly on the ferry, cannot be left to one responsible person. Make sure you travel only with staff who are aware that they are never off-duty. On the coach, have staff sitting in the body of the coach as well as at the front. In town do not disappear from view. If you and your colleagues are having a meal together, do it in a prominent place. Or take it in turns to have a meal in pairs choosing a restaurant where you can see and be seen. Above all, never fail to count before you leave each stopping place. Count twice or have a colleague count after you. *Never* ask children if someone is 'here?'. It is perfectly possible to leave without one of your party, believe me! Sharing the load with colleagues who will 'be around' can go a long way to relieve you of stress about such things as behaviour, accident and (the teacher's nightmare), 'the lost child'.

(2) Consider your position 'in loco parentis' and be realistic about it. This concept can be a great worry to teachers. It sounds daunting. But don't let it ruin your peace of mind. Accidents and illness *will* strike occasionally on any holiday. Get rid of the idea that you can prevent anything untoward ever happening to any of your party. Like the average parent, you cannot. Think about what 'in loco parentis' actually means in law. Legally, you are only responsible for an accident if you did not take the precautions that any normal parent would have taken. Are you likely not to have done so? In fact, you are likely to have done more. Make rules which are firmer than the rules you would make with your own family (e.g. no swimming), and be around to see they are not flouted. 'Being around' is important in two ways, not just because you can see what is going on, but also because you will receive valuable information from children about what is happening/has happened/is about to happen elsewhere. They will tell you who is unhapppy, who has had their purse stolen and who has bought firecrackers. As long as you are available. They are the people who really have their finger on the pulse, but they will not come into the cafe to tell you about it …

(3) Good preparation. Talk to the children before you go about things that may go wrong and what action you expect them to take in order to avoid them. You will develop all sorts of small strategies for them which make things go smoothly e.g. collecting all the passports so that none can be lost, insisting no child goes round the town in a group of less than three, explaining that ferries leave whether your coach is there or not. (Long before you go, they should be aware that being late at coach stops is not an option.)

(4) Be aware that there is a hidden safety net beneath a school party should the worst happen. It is called 'the community'. *Everyone* feels responsible for a party of schoolchildren in difficulties. Even people like the SNCF. An experienced trip leader will have had almost every conceivable accident or illness happen to the children in his or her care. The same resources will swing into place abroad that would be available at home (doctors, hospital, the police), the only difference being that you take the place of the parent.

You can always rely on a French packed lunch

I only became aware of this supporting network when waiting to cross the Channel from the South of France during a ferry strike. First the ferry was leaving, then it wasn't. The train dropped us all off on the dock and hurried back to Paris. We waited. All around us seamen were running around holding agitated meetings. Was the ferry to be allowed to sail, or wasn't it? I would have preferred the group to look pathetic and lost, so that the ferry crew would worry about us, but not at all – they loved it. It was a hot day and another unexpected few hours in France. We did not have the comfort and security of a coach, but it didn't matter. We sat on the harbour wall surrounded by our luggage, basking in the sunshine. Food was not a problem. It goes without saying that we still had the remains of the packed lunches given to us by our families. Anyone who has experienced a French packed lunch will know what I mean. (Six hard-boiled eggs per person goes a long way). The children were looking forward to an adventure. I was not. I was too busy worrying about our train reservations from London, and where we would spend the night if we had to stay in France. I rang my French colleague who had seen us off earlier that day. 'Don't worry', he said, 'the town will find you somewhere. They'll open up a school for you or something'. I felt that he was right. A group of schoolchildren would be seen as the general responsibility of the community. The anxious party leader in me subsided. In the end, the ferry decided to sail after all. (I don't *think* it was anything to do with getting our group out of the country as quickly as possible.)

Stamina and an optimistic outlook

We managed to cram ourselves onto a train at Dover, but of course when we arrived in London the seats we had reserved for our onward journey north were a thing of the distant past. At King's Cross all the trains were full. It was the middle of the night and the children had been travelling for more than 24 hours. They rose to the occasion. (They always do.) I threw myself on the mercy of British Rail (as it then was). The stationmaster was magnificent, doing everything in his power to help us on our journey. Officials of road, rail and sea (and no doubt air as well) are united in their attitude to school parties – move them on! We were found an alternative route and new seats for our journey, arriving home by morning, to be greeted by crowds of relieved relatives. Has such consideration ever been shown to an individual traveller? You need never feel that you are the only person in charge of a school party. As party leader it is easy to imagine, when things go wrong, that, if you don't 'do something', a coachload of skeletons will be found abandoned somewhere in a foreign land. Have no fear, the children do not face starvation and death if you cannot personally get them home. In my opinion, there are only two things you need in this situation – stamina and an optimistic outlook.

Teachers, alas, will be present

There is nothing like the buzz in a school as the day of departure of the school trip draws near. By the day before, it is almost unbearable. Even for the children who have been abroad with their family, a *school trip* has a special magic. For those who have never left their native land, it is an Arabian Night's voyage into the unknown. (Yes, even a day trip to Boulogne.) The excitement they anticipate has nothing in common with your own more idealistic educational expectations, but it is valuable all the same. Because of the wonderful effect it has on the prestige of the language in the school. Children love travel, and after all, students of woodwork don't get to drive for hours in a coach, cross the sea on a ferry (young people adore boats, even the chronically sea-sick …), and have a holiday with their friends and teachers away from the daily grind! If you are lucky, you will be travelling *during* the daily grind. The fact that you are 'missing lessons' is for some the best thing about it and the only reason they are going. There is only one thing about it that is not quite perfect: teachers, alas, will be present. But everyone knows that teachers are different on school trips – more relaxed, more approachable, and *almost human*. Above all, they are not teaching you anything.

Don't worry about motive – get them over there

The children's reasons for wanting to go on the trip don't concern me. Whatever their motives – being with friends, travel, shopping, staying up late, getting away from school/home, having a good time – seeing the country whose language they are learning may not be one of them. This does not matter in the least. Pay attention instead to the few who do *not* want to go. Some of these will be afraid. Think about which of your quiet and shy pupils might feel like this. Have a little word with them, about a friend they could go with, or how some children stay near the teachers all day. A small strategy like this may change their minds, which is important, because these are some of the children you would most like to go. Once there, they almost invariably wander off happily in a group, ignoring you completely. If any child does want to remain close by, that's fine. But the group will usually send in the cavalry to rescue him/her from a fate worse than death!

To revel or not to revel?

I do not subscribe to the idea, current in some schools I have taught in, that the day trip to France is a day when staff decant the coaches into the town and spend the rest of the day in general merry-making, avoiding the children wherever possible. I have seen teachers crouch behind tables when a group of 'their' children pass the restaurant window! It is true that I believe in sending them off on their own, in small groups. I have no desire to lead crocodiles round the town centre all day. I arrange a spot, usually a very pleasant one, where there will always be a member of staff on a rota basis in case of emergencies, and after that, am very happy to go about my business fairly prominently, shopping, dining or sitting on the beach. I do not object if children rush up with news and enquiries when we meet. Far from it, I regard that as part of my function. Apart from the security of having your teacher available if needed, much trouble can be avoided for those individuals you inevitably come across who are (not simultaneously):

(1) paying too much for a 'gold' model of the Eiffel Tower;
(2) desperately seeking the loo;
(3) wondering what time they are supposed to meet the coach (!);
(4) lost.

Language teacher as James Bond

On a school trip to foreign parts, you, and any other adult who speaks the language, will be the troubleshooter. Often there will be only one linguist in the party (other members of the department are either on a course, suffering from a bad back, having a baby, moving house, going to a funeral or did their turn last year). So the troubleshooter will be you. A myriad things can go wrong, and probably will. (Allow for at least one each trip). You are the only one who can sort them out – so be there. On the first day trip I went on with a new school, all the staff retired to the bar on the crossing home to drink to the success of the trip, leaving seventy children of 11 to 13 enjoying the amenities of the huge ferry. This was their tradition and they insisted I join them. But I was uneasy because children were not allowed in the bar and in emergency they could not find us. This did not feel right to me, so after a while, I ignored protests and crept away to do a little tour of the boat on my own. Sure enough a group of pupils, in the process of running around looking for staff, rushed up to me, panting, and informed me that one of our girls was having a severe asthma attack and had been taken away by officers! Where they did not know.

'Sea France' to the rescue

Now asthma attacks are pretty common in schools and I had no idea how very seriously asthma attacks at sea are taken. I tracked her down being looked after in the sickbay, surrounded by assorted crew members, a nurse and, at a distance, the captain! The atmosphere was one of panic. The problem was that she did not have her inhaler with her and really required to borrow one. Unfortunately it is strictly forbidden on board ship to give any asthma sufferer an inhaler, I have no idea why not. I knew this particular pupil well, a very anxious and sensitive girl, and felt that her problem was partly caused by fear and hyperventilation. I had seen her have these attacks at school. Most teachers have asthma sufferers in their classes, and they know the importance of keeping calm. I did not feel that the attack was as serious as the crew believed, and was shocked to be told that they had called an ambulance to be waiting to take her to the nearest hospital in Kent as soon as we berthed. They were very concerned indeed – perhaps afraid that the worst might happen? All this panic and attention, not to mention the presence of the captain himself, had convinced her, not surprisingly, that she was dying.

A new rule is born

She improved as soon as she saw me, a familiar adult, and perked up even more when I told her off for leaving her inhaler at home. Mrs Pleuger obviously wasn't worried, so perhaps she wasn't about to die after all? With difficulty I talked them out of the ambulance, but only by assuring them that our coach would speed to Canterbury the moment we set foot on English soil. (I had absolutely no intention of doing such a thing. If you find yourself in Dover about midnight with a coachload of seventy pupils who have been up since 5am, with a three hour drive ahead, you have only one priority – getting them home! Not to mention the queues of parents waiting to receive them in the middle of the night …). I had a feeling she would make a quick recovery, and she did. The only treatment she required was to sit in the front seat of the coach behind the driver all the way home – glory! A new rule was made the following year – no asthmatics without inhaler. But this is the sort of incident that only the presence of a member of staff and their sheer normality, can defuse. The whole drama could have been avoided if one of us had been there to reassure her when she first became anxious.

In extremis, accept a sweet

Experience teaches that on a school journey *things will go wrong*, ranging in difficulty from the arrival of two police vans, several police cars and accompanying officers (no dogs!) when our group was waiting late at night for parents to collect their offspring on our return (someone had reported a disturbance!), to a day trip lasting 23 hours, involving a breakdown at Farthing Corner and just over an *hour* on French soil! Unfortunately, it also involved thirty or so recalcitrant parents and was the one and only time I ever took parents on a day-trip. For some reason we thought it was a good idea at the time – I have no idea why. Perhaps we thought the parents, clamouring to go with us, would be a help by supervising their own children and generally setting a good example. But parents, I found to my surprise, do not travel as well as children.

Children are the best travellers

Compared with children, parents lack discipline and are generally unsatisfactory school trippers. They do not follow instructions, they arrive late at coach stops, and stay too long in the hypermarket. They cannot be told off when they do any of these things because they always have a good reason, and because they are adults. They have far more needs than children, babies who cry, and inconvenient ideas of their own about what to do. And they do not share their sandwiches. They lose things more, get lost more, criticise staff and fight amongst themselves. Worst of all, they complain a lot. (When you are obliged to wait on Dover docks for 3 hours because you have missed your ferry, the children get out of the coach and play football. The parents moan and groan. To you.) There is nothing you as leader can do to avoid such mishaps, so just be prepared for the odd disaster now and then and accept it as normal. It is not a reflection on your leadership and in most cases there is not a lot you can do about it. So sit down and have a cup of coffee. Accept a sweet from a child. (They give you sweets when they think you are needy). Stop worrying. Although stressful at the time, it was in fact a trip remembered with fondness by an awful lot of children and staff in later years. It was quite a 'badge of courage' to have been there, like the Somme. And, surprisingly, there was no drop in numbers the following year.

To Nausicaa via nausea

Although mishaps like this will occur despite the most careful planning, many others can be avoided. Good preparation is the key, so have at least one evening for parents to come along and be briefed, and have quite a lot of meetings for children before you go. At these meetings you will need to go through with them, and send home, useful details of pre-trip information including what they will need to bring with them. Repeat the same details in children's meetings, parents' meetings and letters home. Hopefully some of them will get through. One important item will be sea-sickness pills for the susceptible, and a bag suitable for its purpose should the pills fail. Younger children will be sick a lot. Who do you think will end up cleaning it up on the coach if they have not brought along a sick-bag? Start building up a large reserve supply months before the day. I was horrified when a notorious nausea queen turned up having taken no pills. I had warned her that she would not be allowed on the trip without them, but she assured me that the wristbands she was wearing would render her sickproof for the whole 24 hours, if not longer. None of us had heard of these magic bands, so we accepted her confident guarantee. Then she proceeded to vomit all the way down to Dover (intermittently), across the Channel (continuously) and all the way home (weakly) until ten minutes from school, when she fell asleep from exhaustion. On arrival, her parents realised that they had put the bands on the wrong way round. The poor girl's predicament was not a problem for the trip as a whole, but it would have been if we had run out of reserve sick bags …! One of the important items to cover at your trip meetings is to make it abundantly clear that supermarket bags with holes do *not* qualify. Also do what you can to warn about excessive consumption of fizzy drinks on the coach. If you are a very unusual person, you may even be able to prevent your passengers, wild with excitement at 5.30 in the morning, from eating and drinking all the sweets, biscuits, crisps and fizzy drinks in their possession before your coach has turned the first corner from school. But I am afraid that is something I have never personally managed to do.

A day tripper's essential kit

Give them early on a list of what they will need to bring with them and make sure they show it to parents. In this way you hope to reduce the number who ring up the day before you leave to ask if their child will need a passport. Occasionally it happens anyway. Other things on the list might be:

(1)   A simple map of Boulogne (toilets marked in red!)
(2)   An itinerary.
(3)   A guide to money values.
(4)   A supermarket bag in which to put their individual litter on the coach. Drivers can be fierce about this, as they usually have to clean the coach themselves ready for the next day. Parties of schoolchildren travelling anywhere are the Olympic champions of litter creation, specialising in bottles. (If you have seen what they can do to the yard in a half-hour break, imagine what they can do to a coach in 24 hours. It is awe-inspiring). Send someone round with a black bin bag at regular intervals, and don't let them get off when you get back until the coach is litter free. However late it is and however tired they/you are. Be brutal.
(5)   Foreign currency.
(6)   A passport.
(7)   A Walkman or quiet game for the coach.
(8)   A camera *and* film.
(9)   A phone card or English money to ring parents. After being subjected to the whole variety of delays to which coaches, not to mention ferries, seem bewilderingly susceptible, I began to revise my policy about notifying parents beforehand of our estimated time of arrival home. I decided that in future, only when we disembarked in Dover, would the children ring home to tell them

what time to expect us. This is important for parents because if we are late they are going to be hanging about at school in the early hours of the morning. You also need to be in contact with a local number which they can ring in case of emergency (theirs or ours), or simply for information. Without this network, you may find yourself taking a child whose parents have not turned up home yourself, only to find there is nobody in.

(10) A watch – to make sure they get back to the coach in time and the ferry home does not sail without you.

(11) A sensible bag (not the schoolbags they bring to school, which tend to be the size and weight of an elephant).

(12) A pronunciation guide (phonetic) for some useful phrases.

(13) A suitable video to watch on the coach – checked by you!.

(14) Some simple worksheets picking out interesting items around the town, or on the journey – for the Head who insists on an 'educational' trip.

The 'educational' day trip?

I am afraid that when your Head speaks of 'educational' he means only one thing – worksheets. I am not in favour of them on a day trip. The truly educational benefit is being in a foreign country and experiencing it in each individual's own personal way. With only a few short hours to spend on foreign soil, worksheets seem to me to spoil the spontaneity of the event and take up valuable time which should be spent soaking up the atmosphere, practising one's French or simply paddling in the (French) sea! For some of the younger children, the beach is the highlight of the trip. It may be the first time they have been on a beach, especially for ethnic minorities. It is a delight to see them playing, and sometimes interacting with nearby French children. On my first trip, I expected my pupils to go round Boulogne conversing happily with French people, using the sheets of suggestions provided by me. I had coached them thoroughly at trip meetings. But I was disappointed. There *was* communication, but not from my sheet. It was a much more primitive affair with lots of English from the French group, a few elementary items from the English group, and lots of body language from both.

'Getting to know all about you'

You will notice that French boys have a way of getting on inordinately well with our girls. This effect occurs without the latter speaking a word of French – or even English. French boys can be something of a revelation to English girls, and no doubt the same phenomenon occurs with other continental youth. I remember it well from my own adolescent encounters. The contrast between English and continental boys at an early age can be dazzling. (Maturity bringing, of course, immunity.) An advance chat about their charms does not come amiss (and especially a mention about the reputation of English girls abroad). On the whole, do not be disappointed if the overall amount of language practised by your party is small, perhaps non-existent in some cases. It was summed up for me when a young Asian girl came and sat next to me on the beach, with something to confide. These are important moments. I had been watching her playing with a French girl of similar age for quite some time. I waited with interest. Pointing at the girl she had been with, she protested: 'Do you see that girl I was playing with?' I looked at the girl, delighted. Only just landed in France and she had already had her first learning experience. What a valuable thing for international relations a school trip is! It turned out not quite as valuable as I had hoped. 'Well,' continued Parveen, indignantly, 'She talks rubbish!'

The compromise workbook

The second time I took a party abroad, I included phonetic pronunciation with my 'phrases utiles' but without noticeably more success. Depending on the ages of your group, you may have to accept little active language input in one day. But think about the passive input – that has got to be phenomenal. Because my Head decided that as we were taking time out of school, the trip had to be more 'educational', I started to give each traveller a small exercise book in which to stick all the sheets they had been given, including worksheets, so that they were kept together, and easy to slip in and out of their bags (folders too cumbersome). I encouraged them to stick in, draw or write anything of interest they came across during their time in Boulogne. I say 'encouraged' in the sense that no-one was obliged to spend time working on sheets or workbook, but there was a prize for the best one. Hopefully giving the impression that we were all beavering away with our noses in workbooks during our short time in France. To give more credibility, I awarded the prize for the best one – and also for the best photo – in assembly. Fortunately some of the keener children worked on their books at home with creditable results. A posse of Year 8 girls usually volunteered to choose the prize in Boulogne, so that it was a genuine reminder of the visit. The only rule was that it had to be suitable for either sex, and also something demonstrably French. This proved rather difficult, because the favoured item was usually a T-shirt or a baseball cap. Amazingly, every T-shirt or cap in Boulogne seems to be printed with a logo in English, which didn't count!

To buy or not to buy?

Now that we have bigger supermarkets in Britain, the thrill of the 'hypermarche' is not so great as it was, but it is still one of the high spots of the trip, for staff and children. Before you set foot in 'Auchan', prepare the children well. There are two important points they must understand. Firstly, receipts must be kept for everything they buy. Hypermarkets used to receiving school parties, are very vigilant and tough with suspected shoplifters. I was once seriously delayed when children were accused of not having paid for their goods and did not have the receipts. Luckily we were able to find them, left on the checkout desk, but who knows how long we would have had to remain there negotiating if they really had been shop-lifting. Secondly, nothing requested by parents involving tobacco or alcohol must be bought. (Lots of parents think 'being a present for them' is OK.) These cannot be brought back by minors and we have no intention of smuggling. Knives, fireworks and firecrackers can also be a problem. Our coach was once searched at the port because shopkeepers had informed customs that our boys had bought firecrackers. (I was not impressed by the morality of first selling them to the children and then informing on them!). By a stroke of luck our coach driver got wind of it, and I was able to confiscate the lot before the search, under threat of abandonment of any boy found with them. (How would their parents feel at having to go out to fetch them back? Would they bother?) Had it not been for the coach driver we would have been caught red-handed. Always be nice to your coach driver. He has done this trip a thousand times before and often has local knowledge you do not. You need him.

Living on the wild side!

An arrangement has to be come to with the party about 'smuggling'. Before this, most of them have no idea about customs, or what is and is not allowed to be brought in back from France by children. You will have explained this to them at meetings more than once, and most of them will have understood perfectly. But in any school there are youngsters who like living dangerously, and there will remain an element who feel that they would like to try it out and see. Being 'illegal' has an irresistible appeal to some young people. Especially as they know they will 'get away with it' anyway. Don't they always? Hopefully you won't have too many in your party. Travelling in a coach gives them a feeling of privacy and security. Wrapped in their cocoon, who will ever know? They never search school coaches and even if they did, and found something, what would they do to school children? Teacher is just being over-cautious and doesn't understand what the real world is about. But 'teacher' has had school coaches searched and 'teacher' does know how strict customs can be with school parties which break the law.

An offer they can't refuse

'Teacher' makes the following contract with them: if they buy anything illegal in France and bring it onto our coach, they are on their own. If it is found, neither teacher nor coach will wait for them. We will carry on with our journey and they will be left in the hands of the police. This contract applies equally to anyone who is caught shoplifting. This announcement will be greeted with a stunned silence, especially by the tougher, older boys. Surprisingly, they are not so much afraid of the police, as they are of being left alone in a foreign country. They have difficulty in believing in such total dereliction of duty by a teacher. Someone will ask, in a shaky voice: 'But what will happen to them, Miss?' My reply is always very firm: 'I don't know. The police will have to send for your parents and *they* will have to deal with it'. This is the most horrifying prospect of all! Being at the mercy of French police is as naught compared with falling into the hands of some of their parents. (I know this from experience of my own). I also mention 'en passant' what the journey to and from France to collect their aberrant offspring will roughly cost those parents. Believe me, they are convinced. If this 'contract' seems rather draconian to you, don't be concerned. It is an invention of my own which I would not dream of carrying out, but it is worth its weight in gold …

Only parents can solve the Eiffel Tower problem

Continue preparation at a parents' evening. Create a pleasant atmosphere by having a video about the area you are visiting playing in the background (hire from the French Tourist Office in Piccadilly). Put up posters and have a good selection of leaflets about the town, especially if yours has a special attraction like the new sea-life centre, Nausicaa, at Boulogne. The parents will need to know how much extra to provide offspring with if they wish them to visit. If your school is less than affluent, it is better not to include such extras in the overall price of the trip. In that way you might deprive some of the poorer children of going at all. Display various items, such as the itinerary, a list of exactly who will be in the party (can be useful for parents to arrange drop-offs and pick-ups), details about money, and all the worksheets and other material their child should have received at school meetings. (Although you will have reserved time at the end of each trippers' meeting in which to distribute sheets to people who were absent from the previous one, check at the very last meeting for the inevitable few who end up with incomplete workbooks). A great asset at parents' meetings are some of those large supermarket advertisements which might have been designed for modern language display purposes, and give parents an idea of what will be available. Don't forget to suggest to them things their son or daughter could usefully bring back as a present. With luck you might cut down on the numbers of dreaded models of the Eiffel Tower which enter the country.

The 'Marie Celeste' of parents' meetings

A word about the logistics of these meetings. They cannot be successful, indeed cannot go on at all, without one essential pre-requisite. Or should I say, one essential person. Not the party leader, not the head, but the caretaker. He is the man with whom you should have a good relationship at all times. Liaise with him. Consult him. Never forget him. Always confirm arrangements made in advance *on the day*. Or you might end up, as I did, with probably the most unsuccessful parents' meeting of all time. How can this be, I hear you ask? Easy! All was well planned for my evening and I arrived early at school. My class had set up the chairs and video in the hall and I proceeded in a leisurely way with my preparations. Although there were prepared screens and lots of materials to be moved from my room to the hall, I decided to make a collage of Boulogne out of tourist brochures, as I had so much time and my Boulogne poster was really past it. I was proceeding in a leisurely way because I had arranged for the help of a colleague and several children at 6.30pm. They were to do all the menial tasks before the meeting started at 7.00pm. I proceeded gently with my collage. At 6.30 no-one had turned up at all. Good job there wasn't that much for them to do. I continued happily with my collage. At 6.45pm realisation dawned – no helpers were coming!

The dawning of realisation

I began to *run* between my room and the hall, clutching materials and pushing display screens wildly along. Display screens are not amenable to being pushed at break-neck speed. I broke out into a sweat. By 7.00pm I was still running and still not ready. But what did it matter? There was nobody there. There were not only no helpers, but no parents either! How rude of all these parents to be late, not to mention my trusty helpers. The thought crossed my mind that no-one was going to turn up at all. By 7.15pm I was in despair. This was turning into the trip meeting that never was. But lo and behold! like a bolt from heaven, at precisely 7.30pm, the hall doors opened and a crowd burst in, a crowd consisting of parents, children and helpers, all indignant. They had been queuing, locked out, at the front of the school. Some of them had been waiting for an hour. I had been working at the back of the school, locked in, and completely out of hearing. Children had been running round the school banging on windows and shouting etc. but to no avail. The meeting, somewhat truncated and less relaxed than usual, took place, and at 8.00pm, just after everyone had left, staff from the travel agency tripped in with their maps, vouchers and customs lists. I didn't ask why *they* were late! And the final touch to a perfect evening – I left my beautiful Boulogne collage in my room, so nobody saw it after all …

The drama of losing a purse

What parents want is information and answers to some of their questions. What you want is all formalities completed and the children turning up with everything they need. Concentrate on the things parents can really *do*. For example, time spent explaining the change of hour crossing the Channel is time wasted. Just make a rule: nobody off the boat until watch checked by a member of staff. Parents will need to hear most of what you have told the children already (perhaps not the 'contract'!) and a description of your destination and what you will be doing there. You can also give useful information about the best deal locally on francs. Sometimes one of the bigger travel agents will be happy to negotiate a special discount for your school, and to buy it back in coins after the trip. Some of them will also send staff to talk about the currency at your meeting if you wish. It is worth ringing round, as many parents pay more than they need by using their own bank. More important than currency, is the issue of passports. One of our girls lost all her francs on the boat going over, and was in tears. We all felt sorry for her because it was her birthday, and she had brought extra money to spend on presents. Some of her friends had a whip round, and of course I quietly slipped her a few francs of my own. She cheered up and had a wonderful day. The day after when we were back at school, she revealed to me that more than one member of staff had secretly slipped her some francs, and she had ended up with more money than she set off with! A good example of the way people in a group come together and give support in 'foreign climes'. In this case having no francs did not constitute a disaster, but having no passport just might.

'It was all in the letter to your parents!'
Do not think that because you have sent home a letter detailing passport arrangements parents will need to make that everyone will now know what to do. Far from it. Letters to parents are subject to almost more of the slings and arrows of outrageous fortune than homework. More often than not, they do not survive the perils of the journey home and if they do enter the house, they lurk for the foreseeable future at the bottom the bag. Which is just as well because budgies become rampant at the sight of one. Repeat everything at the meeting. Explain the procedure and the length of time involved, how to acquire a photo and so on. This is especially important if you work in a multi-ethnic school. Children born abroad will require a visa, which is expensive and time-consuming. Asian parents sometimes think they have to go to London to acquire one, but it can be done through a travel agent. Even those with full English or foreign passports should be reminded to check immediately that they are not out-of-date. Give them a date by which you need to *see* each individual's passport (well before departure).

Don't complain – just remember the good old collective passport
The stress which is involved in ensuring individuals each have their own passport before you leave, is as nothing compared with what used to be involved in that massive edifice. There is not enough space here to recount the complexity of the final document, nor the number of signatures to be acquired by the hapless party leader, including the Head's, on each of up to 70 identity cards (Heads can be surprisingly elusive about these things), nor the photos of children to be stuck on each card and signed by them. Suffice it to say that Michelangelo's painting of the ceiling of the Sistine Chapel must have been a similar undertaking. Posted in good time, with a sigh of relief, one year the passport failed to return to us at school. This had never happened before. We were leaving on May 20th. On May 16th, I panicked and rang Peterborough. They had not received our passport and knew nothing about it! We would not be allowed to travel without a passport and they were sending me a new application form …

A school in crisis

Gloom sunk over the whole school. Everyone knew that the photos, identity cards etc. could not be acquired in time. I blamed myself for not panicking earlier. The school secretary blamed herself for not getting proof of postage. Only the post office and the passport people had no regrets. The trip appeared to be over. Then, as so often happens in crises at school, the day was saved by a leap of imagination by someone in the office. What about taking the photos off the record cards each child came up with from primary school? No sooner said than done. These folders were sacrosanct, and it was probably a sacking offence, but it was done. That's how it is in times of real need. It must have been like this during the Blitz. Unusual people were supportive, even went to great trouble. Nobody in the office thought twice about spending an afternoon carrying out the operation. Nobody minded that some of the children were now *four years* older than their picture! Even the head did not demur at such an asocial act. Nor at the two 'look-alike' photos we were forced to use for the new arrivals who did not have folders. (I use the word 'look-alike' in the loosest possible sense, since none of the travellers looked in the least like their photos anyway …) As for the children, my liveliest classes were as mice for two days, whilst I copied and glued the whole thing together again, a labour of Hercules in itself. Usually unco-operative boys appeared at my door unsummoned, offering to sign their identity cards. The head signed them all at one hour's notice, without a murmur, and colleagues cheerfully covered for me whilst I drove to Peterborough and brought back the final document in triumph, the day before we left!

'In-house' passport control and a crisis of conscience

You are fortunate. With individual passports you can only be involved in individual panics. You can still, however, have a crisis when anxious parents ring up the night before you leave to say that their child's passport has expired. What can they do? Suddenly you have a hard decision to make. You feel like Solomon. Do you tell them their daughter cannot go, or do you risk breaking the law? You know what you *ought* to do, but will you do it? How professional or unprofessional are you going to be? When this happened to me, I am not ashamed to say that I took the girl anyway and we got away with it. I felt the odds were against anyone noticing that the passport was out of date, and that if they did, we would deny all knowledge. If they refused to let her travel, I would stay with her and the coach would go on without us. As usual with teachers, my decision was based on who the girl was, and the effect on her if she did not go. I think I made the right decision, although I'm afraid we failed to set an example of good citizenship to the children.

All-school involvement before you go

The regular children's meetings plus one or two parents' evenings will probably be enough from the preparation point of view. But time permitting I usually ask my class to do a mini-assembly stressing the main points of information, just before we go, when excitement is at its height. A mini-assembly for me is one you do when you have no time to do one. A one-rehearsal job, cast from your class the day before, even the same day in emergency, and read from lines. Extroverts are always willing to jump into these at short notice, because there are no rehearsals, no waiting, no acting and no remembering anything. It's instant. As a way of killing two birds with one stone it works well – reminding the party of what they should be doing, and making the whole school wish they were going too …

All-school involvement when you get back

When you get back is the time to organise a full assembly where more of the flavour of the trip can be communicated to the rest of the school. Those who were unable to go will enjoy it greatly and recruitment next year will benefit. Give some presenters lines to read and performers cards to remind them, and give nobody too much to do. One person, however good, can always be away on the day, so keep each contribution small, simple and easy to replace at the last moment. Beware of being too ambitious – planning and performing an assembly can easily be more trouble than it is worth. Assemblies have a way of taking on a life of their own and getting bigger and bigger, whilst your free time gets smaller and smaller. Try the 'cup of tea in the staffroom' test for stress. (If the CTIS disappears, you are doing too much!).

When Jody missed the coach

By using veteran trippers wearing holiday gear you will have many keen volunteers, but you can cut down on stress by using only your own class, plus anyone who wants to make a special contribution and can do so without help. The audience will be appreciative if you can persuade your colleagues also to wear authentic gear, and everyone, staff and children, to bring in something they brought back, for added colour. There will not be great interest in a more than cursory description of Boulogne, what they are interested in is what you actually did, and any amusing (or shocking) incidents or adventures which took place. What they really want to hear about is the discomfiture of the boy whose alarm clock failed to go off and who was sleeping in bed when the coach left. Luckily he happened to live on the route and was bundled on board in his pyjamas! As far as possible, do not do more than an introduction yourself, unless you have a particularly fascinating personal anecdote to relate. In which case use the 'roving reporters' to involve yourself and other staff. Use your discretion about mentioning something which might cause anxiety, such as the asthma attack. Everything must be geared to the age of your audience.

School visits – the day trip to France

BOULOGNE 14 mai

Départ de Silver Jubilee
à cinq heures.

Sakinder à l'heure
du départ.

Pique-nique délicieuse
- des frites françaises.

Madame Simmonds
à l'hypermarché.

A la plage. Carrie a perdu
ses chaussures.

Kayrene, Parveen et Corrina
sont montées en avion.

Chapter 11

School visits – the exchange

Q How to start an exchange
Q What makes a good match?
Q Why are parents your main resource?
Q What can spell death to a good exchange?
Q Is homesickness inevitable?
Q How do you choose an exchange school?
Q What is the secret of a happy exchange?
A Start with a short, accompanied tourist visit
A Good matching is not the main issue
A Parent goodwill often saves the day
A One in which staff are not closely involved
A Homesickness is natural but can be cured
A Choose staff you get on with and an area you like
A A happy leader makes a happy exchange

How to start an exchange: the accompanied residential visit

If you find yourself in a school where few children come forward for an exchange visit, perhaps because of straitened circumstances in the homes in your area, or because there is simply no tradition of residential trips abroad, you may find an easy way to start such a tradition is to take a small party yourself, staying together in hotel or hostel. The faint-hearted will be happy to embark on such a trip when they would never venture on an exchange. Some local authorities arrange visits like this for primary and middle school children, but if yours does not, organise for yourself a week in a hotel in some delightful spot. Yes, I know this is not exactly your ideal holiday, but it is a one-off thing after all, simply meant to lead on to greater things. Make the sacrifice. I had my eye on St. Malo, but the children had theirs on Paris. In order to qualify for substantial group discounts, it had to be the latter. In fact, Paris turned out to be ideal. Travel and accommodation were relatively cheap, activities for children unending, the summer weather gorgeous and of course, top attraction for the girls – shopping. Naturally, there was little 'mingling' with the French, but there was a taste of French culture, and we hoped that they would all fall in love with Paris, which most of them did. We wanted this trip to be a 'taster' for an exchange elsewhere the following year.

I think you will find a week is long enough

If you are over the age of 25, I think you will find a week of close contact with your charges quite long enough. Make the visit short. In this way you will also keep costs down. For a small group, using a scheduled coach from Victoria is also a good way to economise. Remember that cost can be a big factor in some schools. With this in mind, we booked into the beautiful old youth hostel close to the Ile de la Cité, a tasteful conversion of an ancient building with every amenity, and ideally suited to young people (in-house entertainment all night). There is, unsurprisingly, something very Gallic about French youth hostels. I have noticed it whenever economy has forced me to frequent one. The idea of *sleep* does not seem to be crucial to the experience. On the contrary, the emphasis is on fierce individuality (singing and playing the guitar all night), a certain lack of community spirit (requests from English visitors not well-received), a greater capacity for self-expression (fights and shouting in the middle of the night) and a truly intellectual disdain for the physical (sleep) as opposed to the life of the spirit (reciting poems at the top of one's voice). The lively night-life did not disturb our party in any way, because none of them had the least intention of sleeping, and staff were too exhausted to notice. Most children find hotels and hostels the most exciting places in the world for one or another (or both) of the following two reasons:

(1) they have never stayed in one before;
(2) they can be with their friends for 24 hours a day.

As neither of these factors applied to my colleague and I, we eventually gave up hectoring and pleading by day, or calling out and patrolling by night, and went to bed. It's not as though they were keeping anyone else in the place awake, and we were confident that as the week went on, our intensive programme of activities would begin to wear them out. (Just another teacherly delusion).

We did everything that Paris has to offer

There is no end to the things of interest to do in Paris, and we did them all. Apart from the journey itself (sometimes voted the best part of the whole trip), the most popular venues turned out to be:

(1) The Arc de Triomphe by night, coming up directly underneath on the Métro escalator, the great, gold monster looming above us against a navy sky, flames flickering on the tomb of the Unknown Soldier. (It was news to our party that any other country had had an empire).
(2) Walking the Champs Elysées at night, a fairyland of glowing lights. (Falling asleep on the Métro going back and missing our stop, ending up at the end of the line at midnight). Add to this nowadays the most fabulous summer night views in Paris from the Place de la Concorde Wheel.

(3) Marvelling at Versailles, Marie-Antoinette's cottage and boating on the lake. Sitting dangling our legs in the waterin the heat, until someone noticed the huge carp massing around us, and the size of their *mouths*. Legs were withdrawn from the lake at the speed of light, mine amongst them, with a definite group feeling that they were wanting food, and we might just be it …

(4) Having our portraits and silhouettes sketched at Place du Tertre. (They preferred Sacre Coeur to Notre Dame – until they heard the story of Quasimodo. The bells at Notre Dame seemed to catch their imagination, and when we came back we had an end of term viewing of 'The Hunchback of Notre Dame'. The original version was not available on video, alas, but we made the best of the re-make. (Until you have seen Charles Laughton as Quasimodo you have never really known fear/pity …)

Mainly fun

Where, you may be asking, was the educational element in all this? You are right, it was mainly fun. The two concessions to study were:

(1) An individual diary of events, pictures, photos etc. to be produced two weeks after our return for a post-trip competition.

(2) Hand-outs with historical details likely to be of interest to their age-group, about the places we were to visit each day. Guidebooks on the whole do not hold the interest of this age-group in the same way. The plan was that they would read them the night before each visit, but few managed it, so the relevant hand-out came with us and we would read them as we went along. A better system altogether, leading to questions, laughter and discussion. Because I had written them with that particular group in mind, they actually took an interest, and I am proud to say that some were even seen being consulted independently! The theme of trip was interest and enjoyment. A wonderful introduction to the country was what we were after, and was what we got.

Additional keypoints for pupils
- never go anywhere alone;
- you are representing your country;
- beware of pick-pockets, particularly on the Métro;
- keep luggage light;
- ring home *once*;
- have comfortable shoes.

Exchange visits: a different animal

An exchange visit for children abroad is a different undertaking from the fleeting day trip or the residential visit accompanied by staff. It is longer, usually involves a smaller group, and requires more commitment from children, staff and families in both countries. Accompanying teachers have always had a heavy responsibility of care, and light-hearted staff members who do not understand this aspect of the visit should be left at home. Child protection issues have become more and more important as cases have emerged in recent years of young people being mistreated in their exchange families abroad. Nearly all these could have been avoided with adequate staff supervision and vigilance. Some elements of course remain the same. Things such as travel, passports, collection of money, information giving and communication with parents, do not vary from trip to trip. But the whole thing has to be seen from a different perspective: the selection and care of children and families for a two or three week stay together, in two different countries.

'But does he like rabbits?'

Much attention is given in schools, particularly where the exchange is run on local authority guidelines rather than by the staff of the school itself, to the matching of children with families willing to receive them. Weeks can be spent by staff, sitting in the staffroom clutching forms and debating. Can the popular, sporty boy go to stay with the shy local bookworm? Can the lawyer's daughter fit in with the single parent family of ten? And so on. Staff cudgel their brains to find out which is the most important factor in a successful match: economic status (rich, poor, ordinary?), type of family (large, small, married or single parent?), type of child (quiet/lively, gorgeous/awkward, mature/young for age?). Discussions can go on forever. The children may pick up on what is happening and develop unrealistic expectations.

Sophisticated sixteen down on the farm

Resign yourself to it, most children will not be going to matching partners or families, nor is there any particular reason why they should. The teacherly instinct for order may result in weeks of necessary worry. We like to cover all eventualities and tie up loose ends, but matching school parties is an impossible jigsaw to complete. Unless you have enormous numbers going on your journey, there will never be the perfect exchange for everyone. Even if there were, on paper, no guarantees can be given. Advance matching may appear to be ideal and yet child and host family not fit in at all. And vice versa. I was once obliged to pair a spoilt and sophisticated girl of 16 with a 12-year-old, in the least sophisticated family you could wish for, on a rambling farm with many younger siblings. (The French party did not comprise a single spoilt or sophisticated 16-year-old girl that year) She had the time of her life.

Unconventional pairing: sometimes the only way

She was part of a small exchange party of only 15 or so teenagers which, due to it's small size, had to cope with some quite unusual partners. As the area we went to was rural, social and economic matching of families was difficult. Our school was a large 'country' comprehensive, it is true, but 'rural' in England is not quite the same as 'rural' in France. Our 'farmers' had nothing in common with the farmers of South-west France (Jag-driving as opposed to hay-carting). None of the families presented as single-parent or divorced, and ages varied so much that we considered ourselves successful if we could find a family which contained anyone at all of similar age. If not, we contented ourselves with housing them near an English friend, whose activities they could join if necessary. The temperament of the pair had to be ignored. Totally inadequate pairing, you might say, and yet this was the most happy and fruitful exchange of the many I have been involved in. (See post-exchange assembly accounts below.)

Helping with the pig-slaughter

This exchange regularly involved what might be considered total 'mismatches' of age, temperament, social class and environment. From the British Midlands to the vine-growing area of South-West France! But our children changed and relaxed in the traditional, rustic culture, more open and joyful than their own. The partner was less important because the whole family regarded themselves as responsible for the English visitor's welfare, and there was normally less segregation by age and activity. Fun was expected to be had in the family and not in the town. Cultural differences were profound, but children, even the most spoilt and difficult, can often cope with difference, or learn to do so. If they don't, it is the task of accompanying staff to observe what is going on and help them to adjust. I was often entertained by how well our children did fit in, from the boy who enjoyed giving a hand with the slaughtering of the pigs (!), to the pair of cool clubbers who surprised and worried me when they said they had been at a disco in the town until very late the night before. I had impressed upon them before leaving England that they would not be allowed by their exchange families to go out dancing etc. at night with their friends, but must expect to stay in with their families. They were very pleased with themselves however, and only slightly embarrassed when forced to reveal that they had gone there with their whole exchange family, including grand-mère, *and* had a wonderful time.

An exchange is a joint enterprise

I have organised or accompanied many kinds of foreign exchange, and matching is not one of the major issues. The major issue seems to me to be this: staff on both sides must know the children they are accompanying *and* the parents hosting the return party very well. The better the relationship between English teachers, their pupils and their host families, and the better the relationship between the overseas teachers, their pupils and their host families, the better the whole thing will work. Include your parents as much as possible from the first planning stages and maintain friendly and informal communication with them at all times (letters home) so that they feel part of the thing. I began to understand what this mechanism was and how it works, when I moved from a country to a large city comprehensive, where the exchange was regarded as a formality organised by the local authority, which members of staff were forced to carry out. Because no-one was willing to do so, the system was to ask the most recent member of staff during their interview if they would be willing to organise and accompany the visit. Most felt obliged to say yes. (In this case it was me.)

Know your parents

It was not easy, because I knew neither the children in my party nor their parents, but after our safe return from the visit I was amazed to learn that one of the English families had suddenly decided to take their child, newly returned with his eager French partner, away on holiday and so would not be available to return hospitality! I received this news as a message via a neighbour. I didn't know the family and they didn't know me. I must admit that it came as something of a shock. I knew from experience that finding a family willing to entertain a French boy without any return visit would not be easy. A 'refusing' English family, at such a late stage, was a problem I had never encountered before. I just could not imagine any of the parents on any exchange I had ever organised being capable of such a sudden withdrawal. But this, of course, was the key to the whole thing. As the faces of past hosts passed before my mind's eye, I tried to visualise them telling me, at the moment of arrival, that they could not take the French child after all. I could not do it. There was no way they would have felt able to do so. But why not? What exactly was it that would have prevented them from doing so? After some thought I decided that it was the relationship between us. It would have been 'letting me down'. (Letting down people you don't know is so much easier.)

Parents, allies and saviours

Depending on the goodwill of parents, I have seldom been let down. They have saved the day for the exchange more times than I can remember. An occasion which leaps to mind – perhaps because of the horrendous nature of the problem – occurred when a coachload of French children was being disgorged at school, late one night, after a very long and tiring journey. This was the first leg of the exchange, so that none of the French children had met their future partners or families, and they were arriving in a spirit of some trepidation. (How much harder than the return leg, where the partners know each other). The English hosts were waiting in great excitement. As each visiting child came down the steps of the coach, his or her name was read out and an eager English family, partner (and dog(s)) rushed forward to bear him or her away. Much relief all round. Suddenly, when the next name was read out, there was a hush. No-one came forward. There was silence. Then the host family called out: 'She's too fat!!' twice. I couldn't believe my ears. Yes, this was a very large girl indeed, and it would have been better if my French colleagues had kept me informed so that I could have prepared the family, or found a more understanding one. Then she could have been spared any embarrassment. But this reaction was unforgivable. I took the parents aside and they explained that they couldn't have her because she would not fit into their car! I stood there in shock. Everyone was watching, waiting to see what would happen. The poor girl herself was standing, rejected, on the coach steps. It must have been her worst nightmare come true. Then, before I could pull myself together, another host family came over. Like the Charge of the Light Brigade, the cavalry galloped in to the rescue. They would be delighted to take her along with the girl they already had, no problem. Later they explained that they did it to save the name of British hospitality. I apologised to my French colleagues and went home feeling ashamed.

French exchange without the French

A new teacher should never be in charge of an exchange, for obvious reasons, but there were other examples of bad practice at this otherwise well-organised school. The leader had almost no control whatsoever, all was organised by the local authority, and nothing left to staff. For example, English children and teachers had to leave their host families and partners very early each morning, to go by coach on some visit or activity organised for us. This was something like a visit to a sugar beet factory, or a speech by the mayor. Bike rides, walks, inspection of local businesses, even a radiator factory, filled our days, always as an English group. They were long, arduous days. As far as I was concerned we should have been spending our days with our French partners. Even more awful, when we entertained the French children back home, I was the person obliged to subject *them* to the same treatment. I was astonished. But I found out one of the reasons why our daily round had to be so dreary – no money was available to spend on more interesting trips (London, safari parks, Warwick Castle or Alton Towers). I was obliged to drag them round a tour of inspection of the police and fire station, or any organisation who would have us, walks along the river, and even, unbelievably, 'behind the scenes at Sainsbury's' (with video!) The only improvement I managed to make was to organise a village hall disco for our French visitors one evening, and to get permission from our Head for the host children to take a little time out of school in order to accompany their partner. So at least we occasionally sat on the coach internationally.

Experiencing the 'school dinner'

The dreary nature of our days was not the worse thing about this particular exchange however. Worse still was the fact that we were unbelievably *banned* from accompanying partners to school, even for one hour. I do not recommend exchange children spending days and days in school with their partners, because they can obviously be a distraction, but part of the cultural excitement of these trips is the entry to school of the foreign partners, borne along proudly by their English hosts. Here the visitors can experience an important element of English life so like, yet so unlike, their own, sample a school dinner (unforgettable experience) and chat up English girls or boys on a mega-scale. Our children always talk a great deal about their experience of school in France and I am sure their partners do the same. They will undergo close examination by the rest of the class, many of whom will be doubtful about 'foreigners' and would never dream of going on an exchange themselves. Some will change their minds about that after curiously observing, if not chatting with the visitors at school. They may be astonished to see that French teenagers look very much like, and wear identical clothes to theirs. At the very least they may be more clear about the aims and objectives of French lessons.

'If it doesn't work out, you can always go home'

In my opinion, bad practice occurred at this school because staff did not want anything to do with the exchange and took no responsibility for it. All was organised according to strict local authority rules, leaving no room for friendly, flexible and fruitful negotiation between staff in charge, school, and families. Even control over pastoral care (perhaps the most important area of all) was removed from us. If a child was unhappy, the problem was not the concern of accompanying staff to sort out, instead there was provision for him/her to be brought home with an escort by the local authority! Of course all the children were aware of this and the norm was for one person on every trip to be 'homesick', 'not like their partners' or 'not like the food' and be repatriated. I had never taken children abroad on the basis that if they didn't like it they could go home. It seemed obvious to me that if there is provision for someone to go home, someone will go home. There will always be feelings of homesickness in the first few days and from time to time during the stay.

'I want to go home!': reasons for being 'homesick'

There are four main reasons given by children for homesickness and difficulty settling into the new family:

(1) 'I want my Mum/Dad/budgie'.
(2) 'I don't like my partner'.
(3) 'I don't like the food'.
(4) 'I want to go home'.

It is a quite natural manifestation of two human emotions: separation anxiety and the fear of the new. The younger child or the child who has led a very sheltered life at home, will be the most susceptible. All except the very few will have recovered in a few days. Those who do not will need special help from staff.

The ten-step treatment for homesickness

(1) Make a point of speaking about these feelings in a light-hearted way long before leaving. ('Do you remember when Claire wouldn't come out of her room for two days and Sandrine's Mum had to pass her food in through the window?'). Emphasise the short-term nature of the process to both parents and children, so that no-one will feel guilty or unusual if they experience an unexpected attack on arrival. (It can happen even to the super-cool.) The parents will then be able to cope with homesick phone calls without too much anxiety. Watch out for parents who suffer from 'homesickness' for their child, and miss them terribly. They inevitably pass on their feelings to son or daughter (usually daughter), even before the group leaves, and can make settling down particularly hard. They may even feel they are letting their parents down if they are *not* homesick!

(2) Make sure that those who have done the exchange before, been homesick for a time, and yet ended up not wanting to go home, get to talk about it informally with the rest of the party at some time before departure.

(3) Explain that homesickness is a normal reaction to first-time foreign travel and that adjusting to new surroundings, alone, and without the support of parents, is one of the many skills they will take back with them when they go home.

(4) Make sure to bring up the subject after arrival and encourage talk amongst themselves, because some young people prefer to be homesick in secret. The others will all be aware if anyone is bottling anything up or secretly miserable.

(5) Sincerely congratulate those who are *not* homesick and thus encourage those who may be to follow suit.

(6) If improvement is slow, and you have not yet done so, make a home call, without making it obvious why you are there. I make a practice of visiting all the children at least once during our stay, more if necessary. Very enjoyable these visits usually are, too, if you have taken the precaution of exchanging with a school in a wine-growing area. I was once near Reims, where each family welcomed us with, not cups of tea, but tumblers of champagne. It would have been rude to refuse, of course. How amazingly convivial the atmosphere was on these occasions, how 'cordiale' the 'entente' (and how many more visits seemed to be needed). If the visitor is feeling isolated in his/her new family, I have always found that other children are the best cure. Visits from friends as well as teachers, or perhaps the sharing of activities with an English friend nearby, can nearly always make things bearable. I have noticed that sometimes the worst sufferer turns out to be the one who in the end enjoys the visit most in the end, and is the most reluctant to go home. Maybe because s/he has a tendency to make deeper attachments in the first place?

(7) Make sure you have a good relationship with all your pupils. They must feel able to confide in you, to voice their feelings and not bottle them up. (This is

particularly important in view of current concerns about mistreatment of exchange children abroad). No pupil, of any age, should be isolated in their host family. If you are called to a house where the English child is crying all the time but will not say why, her host family will be depending on you to find out the reason. But s/he will not talk to a teacher s/he hardly knows. Forget about school, in this situation you are taking the place of the missing parent. I was once called out by the family of a girl who wasn't eating anything. The French find this especially threatening and her host family was distraught, fearing her imminent demise. (I have seen grown men cry when their English guest won't eat the wonderful food prepared for them). I took her up to her room and we had a little chat. She seemed fine, healthy, not particularly homesick, just not keen on the unfamiliar cuisine. We had talked before leaving about what is different about French food and, more importantly, what is the *same* (e.g. chips, eggs, bread, tomatoes, yogurt, ice cream, fruit, potatoes, some vegetables, salad, many desserts and much more), and she was quite clear that there was much that she could and should be eating. That was not the problem. She had a secret and wanted to tell me about it. It was under her bed. Would I like to see it? I was intrigued. Had she smuggled in her pet rat? Had she been shop-lifting? Hiding a dead body? What on earth could it be? I watched fascinated as with enormous pride she dragged out from under her bed the biggest bag of chocolates, biscuits and sweets I had ever seen in my life. Her parents had thoughtfully provided her with this lifesaver after hearing about French food. They were confident that she would not eat it, and had hit upon this as the only way of saving their (only) child from starvation. After all, 'she was such a fussy eater'!

(8)   Encourage contact with home, making sure the parents are available and that there is no practical problem, such as money, dialling codes etc. (The host family can help here). If homesickness is interfering with family life, (e.g. still crying after twenty-four hours), ensure regular calls from home, perhaps having a quick word with the parents yourself explaining the position. This is usually frowned upon on school exchanges as an invitation to the child to be even more attached to their family at home. But I take the view that if the cause of the upset is 'separation anxiety' then the best thing to do is to lessen the separation. I have found that homesickness sufferers on the whole feel more secure when they know that their parents are available on the end of a phoneline, and will probably ring less often.

(9)   If things do not improve, and there seems to be a clash of personalities with the partner (very unusual), a change of family may make a difference. This is not always the best solution and should really be a last resort. I have been forced to do this only a couple of times and both were for boy/girl pairings, which seem

to be more fragile. (When they work, however, they can work spectacularly well).

(10) Work very closely with your host colleagues at this stage. Emotions can run high when a visiting child changes family and feelings of 'rejection' are inevitable. Not to mention competition between old and new family. Be in close contact with the family s/he is leaving and take full responsibility for the decision. Make sure they know that you appreciate all they have done and that the outcome was not their fault. Apart from considerations of common courtesy (host families in this situation have usually worked and worried very hard indeed), your colleagues may need to call on them next time!

The final solution: brush up on your Monopoly

Of course, if all strategies fail and one of your party remains deeply unhappy, the final solution must be implemented. This is not something I recommend and have only experienced it on one occasion, and never with one of my own party. After much deliberation, my French colleagues and I decided that a very unhappy French girl, who had changed families twice, would have to move in with us. She settled down at once with her familiar teachers and enjoyed the rest of her stay. But it is not a good solution and one to avoid at all costs. For her, living with familiar teachers from home took the 'English' out of the 'English exchange' and it became just a 'trip to England' She had a very happy time. We did not. Mainly because the French teachers felt obliged to do their duty by investigating British culture in depth in the evenings (at the pub), leaving only one person to stay in and play Monopoly – guess who?

Diplomat, doctor, child psychologist, parent and friend?

The ultimate success of any exchange visit depends on the support given to children and families by accompanying members of staff. (There has been publicity in recent years about cases in which young people were not given this care ...) He or she will need all the above skills, plus a few more (nutritionist? clairvoyant? paramedic? escapologist?). But don't worry, choose a reliable colleague with whom you get on well to share the load, and feel that between you, you can cope with anything. If you are starting from scratch, keep looking until you find a school to exchange with which suits you (city, small town, mountains, sea, country?), at a distance which suits you and with staff who suit you. Take advantage of the fact that teachers abroad are very keen to find English-speaking schools to exchange with, and you will have a wide choice. 'The Central Bureau for International Education and Training'[1] will help. If your school has an established exchange which you find unsatisfactory, don't hesitate to drop it and find another. If you are not in charge, talk other people into doing so. It is important that you also enjoy your exchange trip. If you like skiing, go to the mountains, if you like wind-surfing, go to the sea. This is not self-indulgence. Pupils also enjoy these things. It is a way of ensuring that you keep going back, year after year, so that long-term links can be established between families, children and staff.

How to find the right exchange school for you?

You will need to look for:

(1) Colleagues abroad who share your own methods and outlook and are reliable. (Remember that other European teachers may not be accustomed to the quite the same pastoral role as British teachers).
(2) Colleagues you find easy to entertain in your own home.
(3) A school in an area which has lots to offer both to you and your pupils. This may not mean in a similar area to your own.
(4) A journey which will suit your groups in terms of cost and length.

A happy leader makes a happy exchange

Once found, it will go on for years. It has a flavour all it's own, with the same people visiting year after year, familiar to all. Our school grew to know the French staff almost as well as their own. For those who had never travelled, knowing them by sight was reassuring and encouraged them to take part. Some parents made friends with their child's host family and visited independently. Staff, who may have started by acting in the interests of the department, found their lives enriched also. If you are lucky enough to have found exchange colleagues with whom you have much in common and whom you enjoy entertaining, they will become almost family over the years, relationships which may continue for life. Not to mention the language and professional advantages of having a permanent base abroad.

Additional keypoints for pupils:

- arrive with small presents for your host family;
- smile, and talk to your hosts;
- help about the house; say 'merci, 's'il vous plaît' and 'c'est bon!';
- try any new foods; *do not complain* about anything;
- show interest when shown the sights (smile, ask questions);
- do not smoke;
- do not make comments in English thinking you will not be understood;
- write a letter of thanks on your return.

Note to Chapter 10

1. Central Bureau for Education and Training, 10 Spring Gardens, London SW1A 2BN.

Accounts written for diary and used in post-trip assembly

(1)

Last summer I had the pleasure of going to France on a school exchange. I always thought school exchanges would be dull but I was glad to be proved wrong.

It took 25 hours of travelling to reach are destination but all this added to the excitement of a trip to the South-west coast of France.

The 12 or so days I spent in France drifted by in a haze of happy memories like the day we all spent playing volleyball at the lake, and my great experience of flying a plane from Cordouan to La Rochelle and my pathetic attempts at wind-surfing. I wasn't the only one to fall in.

School exchanges are a good idea and I hope they keep up this great idea.

Jason Cartwright

(2)

Listen very carefully, I shall say this only once!

I went on the Bordeaux Exchange last year during the summer holidays. I stayed with the Richard family. Karine was my hostess. She had three brothers and four sisters. Karine was the 4th youngest.

When I first met my family they were so small that they only came up to my shoulders and me being tall gave the dad an heart attack. I say 'bonjour' and feel really chuffed. Then the French kissing, one peck on each cheek alternately 4 times then doing that 40 times was overdoing it, I felt dizzy and had to put my head between my knees to resuscitate.

My family were baton-twirling Morris dancers, I could twiddle too and then I nearly killed everyone in the family. They had 18 cats and 5 dogs and with them barking and miaowing every minute of the night I didn't sleep very well.

I loved the French meals and I ate it all up. I saw many sites of Bordeaux and Pauillac. In all I had a great time.

Debbie Parker

Chapter 12

The four skills: listening and responding

Q Why the human voice?
Q What can be done to avoid 'tape panic'?
Q How can you slow them down and make them think?
Q 'Challenge' or differentiation?
Q Can listening be fun?
A Your live and familiar voice is easier to hear and gives confidence
A Give pre-tape hints to help comprehension, short segments and extra repetition
A By refusing to reward speed, and by penalising those who 'jump to conclusions'
A 'Challenging material' in the early years may destroy the confidence of the majority
A Yes, if your material is of interest to the learners, at their level, involves an element of choice and is always light-hearted

Stage 1: Starting with the human voice
(1) Begin with simple picture lotto.
(2) Progress from individual words to phrases, then sentences, then longer pieces.
(3) Introduce questions in English one by one orally, to avoid any reading or comprehension problems. This is also a good way of checking that everyone knows what they are listening for. When learning something new, it is important to introduce only one skill at a time, and for that reason it is wise to use questions in English for beginners. If questions in FL are introduced at a later stage, unnecessary confusion will be avoided.
(4) When all the class have acquired the skill of listening for information, remove the visual stimulus, but not too soon.
(5) Proceed at the speed of the slowest.
(6) Use the human voice until they are confident about what they are doing and ready to move on to tape. The taped voice is very much more difficult to follow than your own, not just because of speed and unfamiliarity, but because it lacks the infinite variety of signals which human beings use to communicate face to face, involving intonation, energy, breathing, body language and many others of which we are not aware.

Stage 2: When ready to move on: getting over 'tape anxiety'

(1) Use a slower-than-authentic beginners' tape which is clear, loud and distinct.
(2) As a means of reducing anxiety ('I can't understand a word!') describe roughly what is going to happen in the passage before you start. Suddenly hearing a block of strange language can be very disorientating.
(3) Play a few words to start with followed by a simple question e.g. 'What is the girl's name?'
(4) Play the fragment until all have understood.
(5) Hear oral answers.
(6) Repeat.
(7) Increase the length of the segment gradually and strictly according to the tolerance of the class. (This is a fun activity!)
(8) Create a success situation by avoiding 'tape panic'. This occurs when the speed of the passage exceeds the speed of comprehension of the listener. If necessary, give help with the question, break down material into shorter segments and always, always give as many repetitions as required.
(9) Most learners enjoy listening work as long as they can achieve some measure of success. If this is to be possible you must remove the idea that anything less than full marks is failure. Set them the target of getting half the answers correct (maybe more depending on the general level of ability of the class). Try and keep that proportion as the norm for each piece of tape work and make it clear that it is a satisfactory result. In this way they can succeed whilst still making a certain number of mistakes. This will relieve the pressure and enable them to feel good about their work.
(10) If some children are becoming anxious, or failing, go back to the previous level of difficulty.

Stage 3: Making them think

(1) When the class is very confident with this method and want to do written answers, repeat Stage 2 maintaining exactly the same level of difficulty.
(2) Learners write their answers and mark each others'. It is important to establish self-marking wherever possible and in this way avoid teacher stress. An activity which does not involve teacher marking can take place at least three times more frequently than one which does.
(3) Make it clear that getting all correct answers is not expected.
(4) Be aware that some children may perform badly because of poor hearing and be on the look-out for them. Move them closer to the cassette player and report the difficulty to their Head of Year.
(5) Find a way to make them think. Give lots of time for decision making and make it clear that this is what the time is for. Give them as many repetitions as they need. Hopefully in this way you are slowing down the 'I've got it!' type of

young listener. His style (it is usually a boy), is to make sense, instantly, of the first fragments he hears, in one great imaginative leap. It does not matter too much what sense. This is an admirable ability which can be of great use at a later stage, and it may be the way it which we do our first listening as babies, but it is not what we are looking for here. Without help now, he is in danger of becoming an *old* listener using the same technique. Slow him down in any way you can. When you see the light in the eye and the waving hand on the first hearing, make a 'dramatic gesture of horror' of your own choice. If this has no effect, shout 'Think!' Do not go on until the hand is down and he has given visible proof of thought, whether genuine or not. (It is unlikely to be genuine because he has already made up his mind). Wild guesses seem to rule out subsequent banalities such as further listening. But this race is not to the swift, it is to the correct. At least he is forming the habit of waiting, and hopefully sheer boredom will in the end force him to engage with the tape again.

A dramatic gesture of horror

You may be wondering about what constitutes 'a dramatic gesture of horror' (not to be confused with 'a dramatic gesture of rage'). I cannot tell you. It is a very personal thing and only you can know what form it will take. It must come from the heart. Find out by trial and error what works for you. (It must terrify all present). Use it only 'in extremis'. As a teaching technique it can succeed where all else fails. Use it when patient hours of explanation have fallen on deaf ears and the clearest instructions and hours of practice have proved fruitless. (A good example of the effective use of this kind of body language is a GCSE oral candidate I once had who *for five years* persisted in pronouncing the 'p' of 'beaucoup' at all times, despite otherwise reasonable pronunciation and my best efforts. Two weeks before the exam, he continued to do so, to my intense irritation. I know that in the great mark-scheme of things such a minor failing is of little consequence, but this was an intelligent boy. I will not reveal what I did to him in a final one-to-one practice session, but the offending 'p' departed from his repertoire at once and forever. Suffice it to say that my 'dramatic gesture of horror' involved violence, but it *was* legal!

Stage 4: Differentiation
(1)   Repeat stage 2 but using a slightly more difficult tape. However it must still be slow, clear and distinct.
(2)   Differentiation may be begin to be appropriate from now on. Avoid feelings of inadequacy for some by providing question sheets at two levels, maybe more later. Check that all questions have been understood. Let the student choose which level to attempt. At all costs, do not differentiate by outcome – too depressing!
(3)   Here you may find that your course progresses too quickly on to more chal-

lenging and faster taped material. Do not be tempted. This is a very quick way to destroy learner confidence. Avoid it for as long as possible. A single passage which cannot be understood may be enough to convince a learner that they 'cannot do listening', with disastrous results for future concentration. Unearth your discarded courses and use their often excellent tapes. In this way you will have a wealth of material at all levels. It is vital not to move on to passages which are too difficult too soon, as they cannot be successfully differentiated.

Stage 5: Working towards GCSE
(1) Continue at this level for as long as possible.
(2) Teach FL questions and answers gradually and with care. Phase them in, one at a time, amongst the English questions. Introduce a certain type of question, for example 'pourquoi/parce que', on its own, and use *no other* until it has been completely assimilated.
(3) Gradually increase the difficulty of the passage and questions and decrease the number of repetitions.
(4) Only you will know how far to go down this particular road. Your task is never to lose the majority, and you can do this by differentiating by task and not outcome.
(5) Hopefully, as GCSE approaches you will be able to segregate foundation and higher candidates. In this case your differentiation problems are to some extent solved, and you can have groups working happily and to the best of their ability at a low or reasonable level, plus a really proficient group or groups who will be working with:

Stage 6: Ready for the exam
(1) authentic French
(2) at authentic speed
(3) with few repetitions
(4) and difficult FL questions!

Fun activities for listening
Use of target language in the classroom
Comprehensible FL instructions and comments by the teacher in the classroom make listening skills particularly meaningful and relevant and you can have a lot of fun introducing them (see Chapter 15). Bring in this language slowly and gradually and only at the speed at which the class can digest it. Confusion about what is going on can be destructive, and discouragement can be great for those who are left behind.

Vocabulary
All your vocabulary learning work can be designed to exercise the skills of both listening and speaking (see Chapter 4).

Singing

Singing is a tremendous aid to listening (see Chapter 17). Songs are fun and should not be presented as 'tests'. If they are enjoying them, the children will naturally look for meaning. You can start by helping them to pull out what they can, in an informal way, without spoiling the spontaneity of the music, even if it is only one or two words. To translate straight away deprives them of an opportunity for mastery. Of course, in a beginners' song like 'Frere Jaques' there will be no input from the class (except perhaps the bells!) and you will translate, unobtrusively, as you go along. However, a song will be of no use for listening unless they are fully aware of the meaning of what they are singing. So make sure they copy out the whole thing in both languages, with illustration (excellent folder work for relaxation), and check periodically for meaning. But not before they have thoroughly enjoyed the performance. In this way there will be a constant conscious or unconscious matching up of the two languages for meaning every time it is repeated. (Who could sing 'Douce nuit, Sainte nuit' a few times without wondering what it meant?) Valuable things also will be learned about how far you can, and cannot go with this particular kind of translation. Repetition is the most valuable aid to learning, and a popular song which the children love will provide it endlessly. You will notice also how well children pick up quite difficult pronunciation from FL songs. Repetition is also important for memorisation. New mothers trying to soothe their infant to sleep are sometimes surprised by the unexpected – a sudden outflow of lullabies and baby-soothing songs they had no idea that they knew. These songs must have been lurking in the unconscious, totally 'forgotten', for twenty, thirty years or more!

Games

Games can be another fun way to improve listening skills. Most of them contain an element of listening and there is something for everyone available from excellent publishers, especially Mini-flashcards Language Games.[1] (Start with the 'Resource Pack' including eight packs of cards and branch out later into 'Groovy Grammar Games' etc.) Before really good games came onto the market I used to make my own, but they are never as attractive and exciting as the commercial product, which the children prefer. Invest part of your meagre capitation in some entertaining games (try them first, perhaps at CILT). They are more successful and far more motivating than most worksheets. When playing a game with friends, just for fun, the pressure is off, and this makes it an ideal learning situation. Each time a player asks for a card in a simple 'Happy Families' – type game, the brain will register the sound of that word at the same time as it registers the visual image. The two together form a powerful trigger for learning.

Individual tape work

If each learner can bring in their own tape, much fun can be had with both listening and speaking:

(1) Children *love* setting 'tests' for other people. Pairs or groups can record listening passages for other pairs or groups and swap. Or for the whole class/other classes.

(2) Children record each others' personal information (to avoid voice recognition) for another class to guess who's who.

(3) Two classes learning the same song make a recording of their performance and compare.

(4) If you can buy abroad one or two of the delightful 'listen and read' books of fairy tales etc. accompanied by a cassette, these can be at just the right level for a keen pupil to take home, listen to and report back on (with or without the reading). For the more advanced, 'Livres Cassettes Folio Junior' (Gallimard Jeunesse) can now be obtained over here, of which the most accessible is Antoine de St. Exupery's 'le Petit Prince'.

Teacher tape work

Above all, do not restrict yourself to formal materials but *make your own*. There are no limits to what you can concoct on tape. Make it as personal as you can e.g. you describing other members of staff for the class to guess, your new dog, the story of some event on the school trip, or at the school summer fête or disco. Like the FL newspaper, it can be closer to the children's lives than any course you are following, and whatever it is, it will be far more fun.

Films

If you can find suitable FL films which can really engage your classes then you have an ideal listening exercise, not to mention window onto the culture of your foreign country. But the film must be of great interest to the viewers, with sympathetic characters and action suited to a young audience. Finding such films is not easy. Not all the classics are suitable for a classroom audience (!). My most successful films were recorded from television: 'Les Cases Nègres', about the struggles of a young Caribbean boy to acquire an education, 'Maître d'Ecole', about a young teacher's first efforts in a village school, and 'Henri', about a teenager running away from home after the death of his mother. Pupils connected to the universal human emotions involved, and the films went down very well starting from Year 7/8, and were greatly looked forward to as a form of light relief, in short instalments each week. To maintain their appeal, there were no formal worksheets, just a few questions from me at the beginning, and discussion at the end to check what had been picked up. Sixth formers, of course, can learn from a wider selection, specially popular being the famous 'Jean de Florette' and 'Manon des Sources'. How fortunate among modern language teachers we are to have Gérard Départieu as a resource!

Note to Chapter 12

1. Mini-flashcard Language Games, M.L.G. Publications Ltd., P.O. Box 1526, Hanwell, London W7 1IND.

DOSSIER

Les Dames de Midi

Qui est - ce?

Je suis mariée avec cinq enfants: deux filles et trois garçons. J'ai les cheveux blancs. Je porte généralement un manteau rouge. Je suis contente d'être 'Dinner Lady'. Je n'aime pas les papiers partout dans la cour, les enfants qui se battent, et le chewing-gum. Je préfère une cour tranquille et les enfants polis.

Qui est - ce?

a Madame Perkins **d** Madame Proctor

b Madame Whitlock **e** Madame Rider

c Madame Beddall **f** Madame Daniels

ACTUALITÉ ÉCOLE

Lundi le 14 juin 5^{19}, 5^{20}, 6^{17} et 6^{18} ont fait une excursion au Zoo à Whipsnade. Ils ont vu toutes sortes d'animaux adorables ou féroces. À notre grand regret un crocodil irrité à dévoré Monsieur Thomas.

Chapter 13

The four skills: speaking

Q What makes speaking the most important skill of all?
Q How can stress be removed from first attempts?
Q Can role-play be made interesting?
Q Are individual cassettes a waste of time and effort?
Q What exam preparation will be necessary?
A Verbal communication is the most essential element of language our students will need
A Writing and repetition of simple cards give security
A Lively acting, props and autonomy can make it an entertaining activity
A Making your own recordings can greatly extend speaking practice, confidence, and independent learning
A Techniques have to be learned for dealing with exam nerves

Stage 1: Centre stage for the most vital skill of all

(1)   In the days when I learned French at school, it was perfectly possible to gain an excellent grade at '0' level, travel hopefully to France on an exchange, and find oneself unable to utter a word of any real meaning in the language. I could translate excerpts from Simenon novels, and write an intelligent letter to almost anyone, but I could not ask the way to the bookshop. Fortunately for today's students, all has changed and the teaching emphasis is very different. Speaking is no longer the poor relation of language learning, ignored in the corner until a brief six weeks before the exam. It must be up alongside the other three skills from the beginning, if not taking priority. Because the main and most urgent need of a foreigner is not to listen to the language, not to read it and not to write it, but to speak it. Of course the first three are important, but will avail him naught if, after he has listened, read and written, he can not communicate.

(2)   Time is not elastic, and in order to fit it in, speaking must be incorporated into other activities. Fortunately this is not difficult. You can begin by introducing repetition into all your vocabulary learning strategies, especially the flashcard 'tests' (see Chapter 4). Learners will quickly accustom themselves to repeating every new word after you and be hardly aware of what they are doing. As many repetitions as possible will be needed if the pronunciation is to be

retained, and over an extended period. What learners can say today, they have usually forgotten by tomorrow. Be persistent. Repetition has become something of a second class strategy in many classrooms of late, but has always been a valuable tool for learning. (Are you old enough to have chanted your tables in Maths? Do you remember them?). It is the way we learnt our mother tongue in the first place after all. Repetition of the cards each day reinforces speaking skills constantly. And because it becomes an automatic reflex, it is not boring. Also, it takes up almost no extra time.

(3)   Make a joke out of particularly difficult words. For example, should you be unfortunate enough to have the word 'écureuil' in your first unit, do not pretend this is a normal French word which anyone can pronounce with a little effort. Accept the difficulty of the word and join them in their apprehension. You can dispel the fear of failure by announcing that this is a word which is impossible for English people to pronounce and none of them is likely to be able to do so. Tension will be relieved and they will accept your challenge. In order to prove you wrong, feverish practice will take place until someone is successful; more will follow. There is no need to insist on perfect pronunciation by all. Pressure on the less gifted speakers is counter-productive. You will find them making sporadic efforts with the word over time, partly for their own satisfaction and partly for the pleasure of surprising you. At this early stage, the less emphasis you place on perfection, the more likely you are to get it.

(4)   But start the first lesson with a simple pairwork card, (or conversation card, as I like to call them), in order to emphasise the central position occupied by speaking in in language learning. I prefer the term 'conversation card' because 'pairwork card' sounds to me so banal and pedestrian. Also, it in no way describes what is going on, i.e. communication. In any case, 'conversation card' sounds more fun.

(5)   Remember that speaking is the skill about which beginners worry most. Try and relieve their anxiety in the first lesson. Explain that the cards are to form a valuable and permanent collection which will therefore be kept at school in a personal box or container of some sort to be brought from home. Give them the responsibility for this important collection. As well as a practical measure, the box of cards gives a concrete form and shape to a skill which sometimes feels vague and peripheral. The feeling that all this 'knowledge' is going to be contained in one box, at their disposal, helps to create a sense of mastery and control. If given proper status there is no reason why it cannot be in use up to GCSE level, although many students will want to re-organise or reconstitute the format in some way, for instance, using IT skills which they have developed. They will certainly want to recycle their first efforts!

(6)   The task must be very small, and easy to achieve, so that no-one will be intimidated. A good way to start is by having English on one side and the target

language on theother. The simplicity of this is helpful to beginners. When they become more sophisticated, having alternate lines in each language and in different colours is more useful. The card should be attractive and brightly coloured as a stimulus to memorisation. Making the card is not only a useful way of varying activity, but helps the memory process.

(7)   Many repetitions at three or four separate points during the lesson will be needed for confident pronunciation.

(8)   Not all classes will be ready to work on the cards at home after one lesson. If not, give more time for pairwork, or perhaps small group work, when (mixed ability) pairs can be allocated to several groups and can compete for the most progress made. This is a good way to encourage co-operative learning, but will not work for all classes. When they are all ready, send the card home to be worked on, perhaps with family, for homework. Do not let the cards go home until pronunciation is reasonably good. This stage cannot be rushed.

(9)   When the homework has been done, work on the card again in class before testing, and only test when they are all ready. Give all a mark between 5 and 10, and after the first homework, let them keep a record of their own marks.

(10) All homework on conversation cards must be heard and assessed as rigorously as other learning, despite constraints of time (see Chapter 2).

(11) Bring out the card collection for revision at regular intervals.

(12) When they are marking their answers to tests etc., never give the class the answers, let them give them to you, thus unobtrusively practising their speaking skills.

(13) Younger learners seem to find combining memory and creativity confusing, so do not move on to role-play too soon. Conflict between the remembering and the thinking process can be too much! They will be happy practising short exchanges and building up their collection of conversation cards for some time, with nothing more challenging in the way of role-play than a visit to your corner 'epicerie' Personalise it by having them bring their own bag in which to take away (temporarily) what they buy. Try to have all authentic items but beware of leaving real food or drink within. I had some uncomfortable moments when I found one of my Year 5s had been *eating* my centuries-old, rock-hard croissant, encased in polythene for untold numbers of years! He survived the experience, thank goodness, but heaven knows what effect it had on his opinion of French food …

(14) Target language is a small but not insignificant area of speaking which cannot be introduced too soon. Beginning with 'Bonjour' and 'Au revoir' (with a response from them) introduce very simple phrases from the first lesson, but no more than one at a time, and very slowly. Make sure the phrase is understood, by all, and not just responded to, before you move on: e.g. 'Asseyez-vous'. Children are masters of the art of appearing to have under-

stood something when they have not. They spend half their lives doing it. At all costs avoid confusion in the early stages. This is most important for future motivation. If all is not crystal clear, a fear of failure will creep in. Post every new target language item round the room until it is thoroughly learnt, and tested to prove it (see Chapter 15).

Stage 2: 'On with the motley!'

(1) You will find that there is no moment when you say to the class: 'Now we are ready to do role-play!' It will simply *evolve*, gradually and unstoppably, from the work on conversation cards. Natural actors will have 'ideas', and start acting. Others will follow. There is nothing you can do about it.

(2) 'Ideas' are wonderful, but they are not enough. Spontaneity must be combined with accuracy. Although they are quite adamant that they will not need a script, ignore them. All participants will need a script. Even the most lowly non-speaker. All scripts will be written out individually on either card or paper, not only as an aid to memory, and as a way of usefully incorporating all four skills in one activity, but because reading and writing a script, whether copied or invented, is a valuable calming activity. Most important of all, without a script, the star of the show will want to say so much that he forgets half of it, and the worst actor of all, who only has to say 's'il vous plaît' twice, will be too stressed out to come in at the proper time, or alternatively, too stressed out to remember what to say when he does come in!

(3) A simple approach to early role-play is to let the whole class act out the same short scene in several groups, and compete for the best performance, marked by you and the audience. For example, a simple café role-play for early work might involve a waiter/waitress bringing in and offering various dishes: 'Du poulet, 'Mademoiselle?', which the customer repeatedly examines and rejects with feeling: 'Non, je n'aime pas ça!'. Finishing with: 'Oui, j'aime ça! C'est bon!' *or* the waiter pouring the soup over her head. Later they can progress to slightly longer scenes and begin to change details chosen by them. More advanced groups can work out their own scenes on a café theme, and usually prefer to do so (with help when needed).

(4) Whilst we want our pupils to practise the rather mundane everyday conversations which they will need when abroad, it has to be said that buying a train ticket and finding out what platform the train leaves from does not exactly pulsate with excitement. Asking the way to the bus station might be vital one day, and I am sure we have all regretted in our youth not remembering how to say that we can't eat any more (!), but it can all be rather dreary as an ongoing learning experience. But ongoing it has to be, so we must find ways of making it enjoyable, somehow. The fun element, it seems to me, can only come from the *acting* (after all, buying a baguette is not an intrinsically entertaining activity).

(5)   For beginners, start by introducing some sort of physical action into even the simplest exchange, as this helps memorisation, and improves self-expression. For the very first 'bonjour' conversation, include the traditional handshake (kisses later). If the pair are simply ordering a cup of coffee or buying a ticket, an imaginary or real exchange of money, ticket or cup, will help to bring the scene alive for both actors and audience. You will find a few simple props (tickets, bottles, telephone etc.) in the cupboard worth their weight in gold. Once they have seen the contents of your box, there will be no stopping them from adding to it. Holding a glass (unbreakable) or cup in the hand seems to give security to the timid, and mysteriously, pupils are able to transform themselves into Sarah Bernhardt or Sir Lawrence Olivier with the mere addition of a drinking straw. Keep it simple though, or it will become too much of a 'production' and take up time. (I have had to ban girls from bringing in high heels!). You must, however, always be in possession of the most essential prop of all – a tea-towel, to go over the arm of the waiter/waitress.

(6)   If there is nothing very physical about the conversation, (asking the way to the post office, for example), you can improve the acting by giving more advanced learners the name of an emotion to accompany their lines (e.g. exhaustion, fear, happiness), and let the class guess it. Or they can act in the part of some famous character or other (Bruce Lee? the Queen? Superman?). Include both acting and language in the mark you award, and make sure the acting remains only one of the elements in the assessment, because the audience would much prefer it to be the only one.

(7)   I have found that scenes are more entertaining and better acted if they involve some difficulty or problem. For example, the awkward customer refusing food in the restaurant scene above can be extended to include a procession of waiters and waitresses, all with a comment to make in response to his/her 'Je n'aime pas ça!', and other guests can do the same. ('Ooh là là!' is always popular when all else fails and tends to occur in *all* the role-plays). The crying child who cannot be pacified ('Qu'est-ce que tu veux, mon petit?), and the mother who has lost her child ('C'est lui?' 'Non, il est trop grand!') can also bring out the best in the rest of the cast. Give confident older pupils autonomy and a theme, and they will take a role-play and run with it.

(8)   By now the class should have the organisational and speaking skills to work on their own individual cassette, without too much of the 'for-gotten/lost/stolen/hidden/washed/dry-cleaned/eaten by budgies' controversy. (If a class never does acquire the organisation needed they can record their work on a communal class tape. When school finances do not allow, most children can still find a cassette from somewhere and bring it in – even if it means erasing the 'Spice Girls'. On it can be recorded best individual work,

homework efforts, any item of choice, tests for others, etc. Tape recording can be as important for speaking as it is for listening.

(9) Independent speaking should be introduced with care and, in my experience, only in groups who are confident and have achieved a good speaking standard already. Some of the course books rush in far too early, with their many boxes containing alternatives to choose from. Although these boxes were meant to give structure and support to the learner, they can in some cases have the opposite effect and cause stress. Too many choices may result in confusion. For the learner, language should not be some kind of puzzle, but always meaningful. Rather than teach independent speaking, I prefer to let it arise naturally when the learner is ready.

Stage 3: Working towards GCSE

(1) Candidates should be familiar, after at least five years study, with the material they need for the role-play and general conversation part of the exam, leaving only the presentation to be prepared from scratch, if your board includes it (MEG and NEAB). Make sure that those who have not acquired a sufficient repertoire of material realise this fact. Many candidates take a laid-back 'it will be all right on the night' sort of view, and have the happy conviction that the examiner will just happen on the few questions they feel able to answer. Disabuse them of this idea. Give them extra learning to do at home. If they do not manage to do it, assure them of a poor grade. There is no more you can do for them. It is their choice.

(2) There is an element in the speaking exam which is less troubling in the others, and which, any examiner will tell you, more often than not makes the difference between success and failure. And that is: exam nerves. Direct your attention throughout the whole of the final year to techniques for controlling exam anxiety.

(3) What causes speaking exam candidates to be so much more nervous than others? The following are wild guesses only:
  (a) No time to think? ('in shock, so incapable of thinking quickly!')
  (b) Being assessed by a teacher in a one-to-one situation? ('spotlight on me, all alone!') Are teachers so fearsome?
  (c) No second chance? ('silly mistakes public forever!')
  (d) Won't know the answers? ('will be asked questions I've never heard of!')
  (e) Will look like an idiot? ('the fact that I haven't learnt anything will be revealed!')
  (f) Will look like an idiot? ('will never manage to say all the things I have learnt, or even have a complete mental block!')

(4) What techniques can help defuse all this apprehension? Knowing exactly what you are going to do is the key to self-possession. Set up a 'mock oral' regularly

throughout the final year. Let the class hear each other work through the entire interview with you as often as possible. Let them make notes, and afterwards make suggestions about each others' performance. (They are very good at making suggestions about each others' efforts!) You will find that they will learn more from experiencing the 'real thing' than from anything you try to tell them. They will have an idea about what takes place, how long the interview actually goes on (shorter than they expect), typical mistakes others make, how others succeed and how the teacher responds. They can then model themselves on the good candidate. Above all, they know what to expect, and need no longer fear the unknown.

(5) By recording their own performance on tape, they can hear what their weaknesses are (ably assisted by others' comments!), and work on them at home. They should be used to speaking and listening to their own individual cassette at this stage. What are these weaknesses likely to be?

(6) Many will undoubtedly have to work on the problem of speeding ('the jet-ski syndrome'). In their anxiety to get the whole thing over, pronunciation is forgotten and mistakes are made which would never occur in normal circumstances and at normal speeds. Remind this candidate that no-one is expected to reach the speed of a native speaker. Remind him/her about *breathing*! (At the end of every sentence until s/he slows down). As s/he may be able to speak perfectly slowly alone at home, you may have to continue to hear her/his mock oral for quite some time.

(7)) Going too slowly can be just as damaging as speeding. A certain amount of hesitation whilst you are considering your answer can be appropriate, but pauses which become too long are a problem. When is a pause too long, you may ask? It occurs when your examiner begins to feel uneasy and to wonder whether you:
(a) didn't hear the question;
(b) didn't understand the question;
(c) can't answer the question;
(d) have forgotten the question;
(e) have fallen into a catatonic trance.
S/he needs to know the answer before she can proceed with her line of questioning (or call the doctor). And all the time she is contemplating this dilemma, you, the 'non-speaking' candidate, are losing the marks you could have earned if you had been speaking! All candidates, and not just those with a chronic tendency to sit in silence, must have at their fingertips the phrases needed, in these situations, in order to move on swiftly to the next question:
(a) 'Voulez-vous répéter, s'il vous plaît?'
(b) 'Je ne comprends pas' or 'Que veut dire le mot …?'
(c) 'Je ne sais pas' or 'J'ai oublié le mot français pour…'

(10) From year 2001 candidates will no longer have the doubtful benefit of using a dictionary during the exam. Do not mourn its passing, they will manage much better on their own. Think of the preparation time you will save on practice sessions, in an attempt, often unsuccessful, to train them to look up key words only. Think of the time *they* will save on the paper. Candidates are notoriously poor at timing their progress through the questions, and there was no end to the time they could waste looking up necessary vocabulary.

(11) If your board allows notes to be taken into the interview, do not allow them to become another source of stress. It is possible to become 'note-dependent' (so busy searching for help from the notes that they have no time to use the brain!). Confine notes to one-word, or pictorial, reminders. They should be impossible to read out. Reading aloud will be spotted at once and gain absolutely no marks. (This is especially important in the presentation). Cue cards are also allowed by some boards, and need practice if they are to be used. Getting them in the wrong order, fumbling with them and even dropping them on the floor will do little to help with exam nerves, so lots of mock oral practice will be needed in their use.

(12) Explain to the candidates that they may be perfectly confident and fluent in all parts of the exam and still receive a grade D if they do not show evidence of:
  (a) use of past, present and future tenses;
  (b) the ability to state an opinion;
  (c) the ability to construct more complex sentences.
  All these are essential if they are to achieve a C grade or higher, and must be practised from an early stage. The presentation in particular must be chosen with these elements in mind. A presentation is not the easy option some candidates assume, and they must have lots of practice from an early stage with the questions, which will by their nature be unpredictable. The class could helpfully monitor the presence of the above three elements (or their absence), when assessing the mock orals.

(10) In general conversation, nerves will tend to result in the annoying one-line answer. It goes like this:
  Ex. 'As-tu un animal à la maison?'
  Can. 'Oui, j'ai un cobaye'.
  Ex. (waits hopefully)
  Can. (silence)

Explain to your classes why this sort of pause irritates the examiner *and* loses you valuable time in which to gain marks. Why leave it to the examiner to select the next question, which there is a chance you will not be able to answer, when you could acquire marks by saying more about your pet? What you have practised and prepared is bound to be better than anything the examiner can prise out of you. Allow for general conversation nerves by accustoming all candidates to a minimum of two-line answers, which have become automatic, and having a complete ban on waiting to be prompted. Also make sure they can all spell in TL. They may have forgotten.

(11) Finally, practise simple breathing techniques for moments of panic (two slow counts in, four slow counts out is very calming).

Fun activities for speaking
Games

I have mentioned the usefulness of games for listening skills above, and must bring them in again here, because if anything they are even more useful in speaking practice. Games motivate like nothing else. But they must remain a game, if they become 'work' then all is lost. There are two ways in which teachers can take the fun out of games:

(1) By making them compulsory. Learners should only get to play when they have finished work, or as a treat. If games become a compulsory part of every lesson, or are played by the whole class every Monday, they will lose their allure.

(2) By having no margin for pronunciation error in the early stages of learning. I would rather children were speaking French with a few mistakes of gender, or a little ragged pronunciation, than not speaking it at all, which is the alternative. For instance, a player asking for a card he needs will do his utmost to get his meaning across, and if he asks for 'la lion', pronouncing the 'n' English-style, and with the wrong gender, should not be disqualified. He will quickly be corrected by others in the group and learn from them. (By playing for a short time with each group, the teacher can set an example of this process, and model the correct pronunciation for all). I feel quite strongly about this after an inspector reported on one of my lessons that a Year 7 boy should not have been allowed to make a recording for the class, because his pronunciation of the letter 'r' was not good enough. How much fun would we have missed if only people with perfect pronunciation had been allowed to record, and how much learning …?

Drama

Drama, including assemblies (see Chapter 11), will arise naturally from role-play, but will call on far more time and commitment from performers and teacher. The pay-off is not only in language and self-development for the actors, but in prestige for the subject. Read more about 'French plays' in Chapter 6).

Songs

For memorisation, meaning, repetition and enjoyment, songs have no equal in the foreign language classroom. My singing voice is execrable, but even before rescue by the arrival of the cassette player, some of my happiest teaching moments came from sharing 'Frère Jacques' in five parts with Year 5 until exhaustion (nobody ever wants to stop), or 'Dans la fôret lointaine' with Year 6 ('cou-cou-ing' our way round the school for weeks on end. Sometimes parents would complain that they were being driven mad at home). All ages of the school enjoy singing, A-level students just as much, although with different material. For more on this subject see Chapter 17).

Trips abroad

A three week stay with a non-English speaking foreign family is of course the best way of all of improving speaking skills. A longer stay would be even better, if it could be arranged, which it often can for older students. There are organisations which will arrange suitable visits for sixth-formers wishing to stay as paying guests abroad during the summer break.[1] These are a boon for the many households unable to receive a reciprocal teenager. And of course there are working holidays for the more robust. 'The Central Bureau for International Education and Training'[2] will provide details of school travel and exchange, paying guest placements (in both directions), adventure activities, and volunteer work in many countries. (They also organise teaching post exchanges if you feel like a change and can talk your headteacher and family into it. If not, there are refresher courses abroad for jaded ML teachers.) Long visits i.e. longer than the school exchange, can make all the difference to exam results and subsequent university entrance. Be persuasive about this with your Sixth formers and start early, preferably before they begin the course, so that they and their families have plenty of time to gear up. So much easier to get used to the idea of a long visit the year before, rather than 'this summer'. This age-group can be lethargic, and the families fearful. Long-term encouragement from you can often make the difference. Most pupils will not manage either of these stays, and this is where the short trips come in. On a short trip, the speaking practice involved may vary from considerable to nil. All will depend on the individual. But many *will* benefit, and even on the day trip, you will see the most unexpected pupils panic on the coach, and pore over their 'Phrases utiles', muttering frantically to themselves all the way to Dover.

The French breakfast

Eating croissants and French jam is no longer an exotic treat, but it is great fun, and an occasion for cultural exploration and a little language practice. Try and have bowls, instead of cups, so that croissants or baguette can be dunked, and make sure the jam is the real thing. French and English jam are different creatures. Younger learners find this a great treat, even though they are forbidden to speak English. What they enjoy most of all is the fact of being allowed to *eat* in class!

The French fashion show

An Open evening activity can be a parade in the hall of 'models' dressed in whatever they like, and either announcing what they are wearing in French themselves, or being described by announcers, which is more authentic (and easier to prepare). Young people all know how to 'strut their stuff', and parents find it entertaining. The performers will also be only too happy to provide the essential 'loud' music. One important point though: don't forget that when they say 'loud' they mean *'loud'*. You must find someone with very good timing who can turn the music up and down at just the right moment to enable the speaking to be heard. It might have to be you.

The French trophy

If your school has an end-of-year 'award ceremony' which seems to be based mainly on sports and merit points, and leaves most children feeling that these are the things which truly count in the school, think about introducing a small cup, shield or tricolore for the pupil who has made the most effort and improvement in *speaking* French that year. Call it 'The French Speaking Trophy' (or cup or whatever), making it clear that it is not to be confused with general achievement in French. In order to improve the profile of speaking a foreign language in the school, be sure to award it only to a pupil who:

(1)   has put a lot of effort into his/her speaking skills;
(2)   will be genuinely proud to receive it;

Notes to Chapter 13

1.   'Central Bureau for International Education and Training', 10 Spring Gardens, London SW1A 2BN.
2.   'Euroyouth', 301, Westborough Road, Southend-on-sea, Essex.

Chapter 14
Target language

Q What is the aim of the lesson conducted in TL?
Q Can teaching in TL be stressful for teacher and pupil?
Q How can tension be relieved?
Q At what stage should full proficiency be achieved?
Q Exactly what should be taught?
Q What preparation for GCSE is required?
A To encourage learners to experience the TL as a real means of communication
A Unfamiliar language can undermine learner confidence
A By specific teaching and consolidation of each TL item until it is no longer unfamiliar
A Teaching TL should be regarded as a slow process, timed to suit the abilities of the class and lasting many years
A Material cannot be universal and must suit the needs of each particular teacher and class
A Lots of time must be devoted to coping with written paper TL exam questions

Stage 1: Fools rush in!

(1) Conducting a lesson in the target language can undoubtedly be a factor for stress, for both pupil and teacher. (The new National Curriculum thoughts on this subject seem to have mellowed slightly, perhaps in part recognition of our situation, and a certain amount of English may be used 'in a sensible way'). Teachers working in ordinary schools will always find the project challenging, so start slowly. Build up slowly. Avoid confusion. This is not an opportunity for challenge, although it may be later. A lesson conducted entirely in TL is an admirable thing, but must not be allowed to create tension for the uncomprehending.

(2) The aim of the all-TL lesson is as follows:
   - to create an ambience which simulates the foreign country.
   - to help learners develop a sensitivity to pronunciation, intonation, structure and meaning.
   - to enable pupils, by using the TL themselves, to see it as a real means of communication.

None of these aims will be achieved if too much is undertaken too soon. And none of them is worth, in my opinion, the undermining of learner confidence.

(3)   When the use of TL in the classroom was first introduced, teachers were apprehensive. How would we keep the class's attention if they did not understand what we were saying? What effect would it have on discipline if some did not know what to do? Was it wise to interpose another layer of learning alongside what we were already doing? Would the carefully incremental steps of our programme of study be wrecked by the appearance of completely unrelated and unfamiliar (and often more difficult) language, creating exactly the disconnection and randomness we had been striving so hard to avoid?

(4)   However, we went on courses and were told that all would be well. Children would learn by the 'language bath' process, and immediate understanding was not important. It was not necessary for every single word to be understood by all pupils, and in any case the meaning of the language could be reinforced by:

• body language;
• visual clues;
• tone;
• variation in speed and delivery;
• paraphrase.

We were to develop comprehension skills by 'interspersing the familiar with the unfamiliar'. Our apprehension abated.

(5)   all went smoothly for some teachers on their return to implement 'the plan'. Their pupils quickly got the hang of things, saw it as an intriguing 'game', and were able to tolerate the temporary frustration of not quite understanding. Teachers in other schools did not have the same success. My classes at that time, for example, with a very wide range of ability and no setting, definitely did not thrive under the new regime, but became confused and frustrated. In order to maintain language learning as a 'success situation', we had to adopt a rather different approach, based on the following principles:

(a)   Abandonment of the 'language bath' principle, with its clues and guessing.
(b)   Introduction of each target language item one at a time.
(c)   Listening, reading and writing consolidation at the same time.
(d)   Visual 'help' posted around the classroom.
(e)   New items introduced only when the first fully absorbed and in use by *all*. (The child who still doesn't know what's going on will switch off).
(f)   Normal assessment of all TL learning.

(6)   By teaching TL in the same way as any other material, a sense of security is restored to the class. They know they can do it. Progress may be slow, but at the

end of the first year, the class will have a well-used and familiar repertoire of TL about which they are entirely confident. For a very mixed Year 5 class, I would be happy with a short list of TL responses such as:

'Bonjour, Madame, Mademoiselle, Monsieur – au revoir etc. – s'il vous plaît – merci – oui – non – je voudrais une gomme, une baguette etc. – voilà – c'est combien? – c'est tout? – j'ai fini'.

This vocabulary would enable those who wished to use it to hold simple conversations between themselves, but there would be no requirement to do so at this stage. Confident learners who are not afraid to make mistakes, will move automatically into this mode, but those who are not, must feel under no pressure to join them. From me would come the very simplest classroom instructions. There would be no attempt to 'conduct and manage the learning activities in Tl', or to 'use published material avoiding the use of English'. This would come later, much later.

Stage 2: Consolidating the fundamentals

(1) By the end of the following year, perhaps longer, depending on the age and ability of the class, I would expect all pupils to use consistently the following TL:

répétez, s'il vous plaît
je ne comprends pas
excusez-moi
d'accord
c'est quoi en françias/anglais?
excusez-moi d'être en retard
je veux aller aux toilettes
excusez-moi, j'ai perdu mon stylo/livre/cahier

(2) I would be using more managerial language, but only of the easily understood kind (using cognates whenever possible):

entrez
distribuez les livres/cahiers, s'il vous plaît
regardez la page dix/les cartes/le projecteur
ouvrez votre cahier
écoutez-moi, écoutez la cassette
répétez après moi
écrivez 'test' dans votre cahier
écrivez en anglais/français/vrai ou faux
qui va faire les réponses?
vous avez fini?
tu comprends?
donnez-moi vos marques
levez la main

trouvez un partenaire
travaillez par quatre/six
ramassez les feuilles/fiches, s'il vous plaît
rangez vos affaires
silence/dépêchez-vous
au revoir la classe

(3) These happened to be the most frequently used commands and requests used in my lessons; they will be different for each teacher and for each class. It is a good idea to consult and agree what is appropriate with the class, and point out to those who transfer to upper school after Year 8 that they will be expected to cope with the extensive use of TL in their new school. Have them copy a list into an instantly retrievable place in the exercise book (perhaps the two middle pages, if you already use the back for new words). Better still, on a separate piece of card, no bigger than the exercise book. Besides being more to hand, this has the added advantage that it will frequently be lost, and need to be laboriously copied out again! On the card should also be copied the key numbers, for quick reference. (However well-practised and well-consolidated, French numbers continue to be a problem for most English children for years. Whilst they are puzzling over which page to turn to, they are not listening to your next round of TL instructions. You will know this is happening when you see heads turn for a surreptitious look at the books around them.)

(4) General words indicating how their efforts have been received are important, especially if they are mainly applause. In response to something that is really so poor it is impossible to ignore, make a humorous comment, perhaps using body language only. It is seldom necessary to criticise:

beaucoup mieux
bon/bien/très bien
excellent
super
extraordinaire
recommence

There must be some significance in the fact that this vocabulary is the easiest of all for them to learn!

(5) Having talked about the rather dull 'copying of lists' etc. let us not loose sight of the enormous fun that can be had playing games with TL. A good starter and my favourite, is 'Jacques a dit' (the French equivalent of 'Simon says'). The energy used up in a really cut-throat round is prodigious, especially when the whole thing has to continue to exhaustion because the teacher just cannot manage to win! This would be a starter game, requiring only listening from the class, but later on could be extended to have a pupil taking the place of the teacher. When they are ready to speak, have a team game where each side has

to guess what TL is being mimed by one of the other side. Children enjoy mime but are sometimes slow to think of a subject. You may need to step in with a few discreet suggestions to ensure that more than a few participate. Of course, 'je veux aller à la toilette' is always the most popular! (No mime can be performed more than once!)

Stage 3: Working towards GCSE

(1)   After the fundamentals have become second nature, around Year 9, or earlier for some, extension of TL can begin, continuing as far as appropriate for each group, up to GCSE. Following on from the 'fundamentals' developed above, elements to be introduced could be:

(a) Use of tenses:

j'ai oublié mon cahier

je parlais a Madame Smith

je vais être en retard demain

(b) Use of the negative:

je n'ai pas de partenaire'

je ne pouvais pas faire mes devoirs

(c) Addition of an auxiliary:

Est-ce que je peux tailler mon crayon?

Qu'est-ce que je dois faire maintenant?

(d) More use of language between pupils, both for normal conversation and for activities e.g. games:

C'est a qui? C'est à toi/moi. Pardon

J'ai gagné/perdu. Passe un tour

(e) More complicated teacher commands:

Viens me voir après la leçon

Comment ça s'ecrit en français?

Qu'est-ce que j'ai dit en anglais?

Qui veut commencer?

(f) More complicated requests to teacher:

j'ai besoin d'une fiche, s'il vous plaît

comment ça s'écrit en français?

est-ce que vous pouvez m'aider?

(2)   Aim at having a complete ban on English for classroom organisation and activities. Allow body language as the only alternative. In this way you avoid temporary lapses into English, give them the security of potential survival skills for emergencies abroad, and have great fun when you ask the class clown why he is late!

(3)   To the staff of upper schools, as teacher of both middle and upper, I would like to make a request. If your feeder schools transfer to you for Year 9, be sure

to have from them a full list of what TL their children (should) know. Liaison between middle schools on this subject is not easy, and there will be variety from school to school, but continue to include at least part of what your new intake bring with them as far as you can. I know that this is asking a lot, but word will quickly get back to the middle school if they 'cannot understand a word the new teacher says', casting doubt on the value of the learning already done. Obviously it would be ideal if the upper school could provide all their feeder schools with a list of TL which they could then teach. All the pupils arriving at the school would have learnt the same TL. How seamless the transfer would be, how satisfied and confident the children. With this experiment in mind one year I acquired just such a list from the school my Year 8s were going on to. At a glance I could see that the language was far too complex for my particular learners and that any such endeavour would be fruitless. All schools are different, and imposing uniformity in this particular area a pipedream.

(4) Teach the TL alphabet for spelling purposes. For some reason children really enjoy spelling in French, provided they are given plenty of time, and there is much attractive material to use in the newer coursebooks.

(5) Begin to mark written work in TL, perhaps using terms such as:
    excellent
    très bien
    bien
    assez bien
    médiocre
    insuffisant
    très insuffisant

(6) Introduce the comprehension questions used by your examining board and practise, practise, practise. Use them for all work presented to the students in Years 10 and 11 so that there is total familiarity long before the exam. More marks must be lost at GCSE through non-comprehension of the FL questions than any other factor. In the exam situation, normal nerves, panic, or the 'jet-ski syndrome' (must finish the whole thing in three minutes) may lead an otherwise good candidate to misinterpret FL questions, the not-so-good candidate to forget what s/he really knows, and the poor candidate to ignore them and guess wildly. (Can anyone explain how it is that, when guessing 'at random', pupils *never* happen on the correct answer by accident?) The candidate who is always in a hurry suffers most, because he actually throws way marks which he could easily obtain. A teacher of any sensitivity finds this painful. Slow him down, and introduce him to the idea of 'checking' work at the end. This is a concept completely foreign to most learners. Conveying

quantum physics to an elephant would be easier. Have tranquillisers at the ready (for you, not them).

(7) You may be relieved to find your particular board using more simple grids and symbols to test comprehension, but 'be afraid, be *very* afraid'. Remember that although these may appear simpler and fairer than the FL questions, they will pose problems for some learners, especially some girls, who sometimes find diagrams etc. less easy than language. Never take it for granted that visual patterns and symbols have been understood (beware of the arrows!), and practise, practise, practise.

(8) To avoid distancing yourself from your pupils, try to leave a little time at the end of each lesson for a chat in English, not for nothing known as 'the mother tongue'.

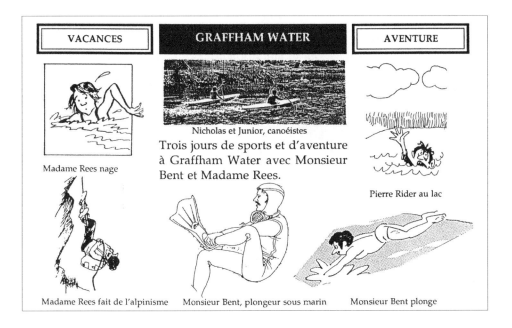

Chapter 15

The four skills: reading and responding

Q Is there a natural urge to translate?

Q Is an independent 'reading scheme' a useful resource?

Q What if my classes don't take to them?

Q What part does IT play in the acquisition of reading skills?

Q What are the most important skills to teach for the exam?

A Yes, and it will blossom if encouraged first by fun opportunities to puzzle things out with no pressure, and later by formal comprehension practice.

A Yes, with a group having sufficient time and motivation.

A Use popular songs, games and other aids, especially IT.

A It can be a more independent, practical and private way of learning, which empowers the nervous and is good for groups (they like it!).

A Total familiarisation with the format of the paper and the most effective approach to questions.

Stage 1: Keep it fun

(1) Reading is in a way the easiest of the skills to fit into your programme of study because it is used so often alongside the other three skills. For speaking, you have to read scripts or notes, for listening, the questions, and for writing, text-books, worksheets, folder work and anything you are attempting to write. However, reading for comprehension must be practised and consolidated as a skill in itself. The learners will be practising their reading comprehension skills all the time, but they will not be aware of it. 'Translation', as we used to call it, fascinates the enquiring mind of the young, especially the more confident teenagers who like a challenge, are not afraid to make mistakes, will risk all on a guess, and enjoy the detective work required. For formal translation, as opposed to competing over the meaning of a cartoon in the school newspaper, or a piece of display work which catches their interest, there is the skill of working out what the thing means, followed by the equally tough task of putting that meaning into suitable English. Often people who excel at one, have difficulty with the other, and I sometimes think the second task is the harder, because it is an art which cannot be taught. Either you know what 'good English' is, or you do not, and that ability seems to be connected with past exposure to reading.

(2) Luckily, direct translation into English no longer features in the exam, but curiosity ('What does it mean?') never dies, and doesn't have to be taught. Young people translate from one language to another naturally, out of interest, whether it be display material, FL pop music, or a penfriend's letter … Encourage this unconscious extension of their language learning ability wherever you can. For example, by refraining from giving immediate help and instead, leaving up difficult display work until they have had a chance to puzzle over it.

(3) Commercial reading schemes devised to support the skills of independent reading are fun, bright, well-constructed and easy to use. The individual reader can work entirely at his/her own pace, record progress him or herself using regular monitoring tests, and proceed entirely independently. This works well for some groups, but unfortunately the process is time-consuming and so does not work too well as a lesson-filler. A whole lesson is going to be needed for a real feeling of achievement, which makes them inconvenient for your average early finisher. (Real high flyers will love them.) Use these readers if you can. But in schools where the pupils lack organisation skills and have shorter attention spans, you may find this system calls for more autonomy and motivation than they possess. What is the alternative?

(4) Learners read best material which interests them. Try to equip them with the skills they need using relevant texts, and incorporate reading comprehension into the activities they enjoy. A quick and easy way to let them flex their translation muscles, is to take a song which is popular with the class, and after translating together and singing, put up the FL words on the OHP and let them translate it again for you. Orally, as a class. Whilst writing out their own translation would be stressful for some, whole-class translation can be fun for everyone. It is mixed-ability, and can be used to translate absolutely anything. It is very fast and completely stress free, because it is a corporate endeavour. Learners call out whatever they can, including guesses for the bits *no-one* can remember (it's no fun if they know it all). To keep up the speed and the suspense, you may have to help out here and there at first, but the more skilled they are the less you should intervene. Let them keep on guessing. Give them time to puzzle and to champ at the bit, racking their brains and wondering: 'doesn't *anyone* know it?', 'come on somebody!' Teach them the technique of leaving the difficult word until the end and coming back to it, a very important skill which children are not good at. Give the occasional clue if you think they deserve it, and only when all else fails. Less adept translators will see others using the basic skills of translation and be able to learn from them. But the beauty of it is that surprising items can be contributed by the most unexpected people. What a glow for the usually poor translator who was the only one in the

class to know (or guess), the word! Dividing the class into two and making it a team game, will hot things up considerably, of course.

(5) 'Stile' trays, known as 'self-checking vocabulary consolidation resources using the LDA Stile Tray'[1] are invaluable for early independent learning in the first years, particularly because they are regarded as a game. You cannot have too many of them. Each learner has a tray containing twelve attractive pictures, twelve numbered tiles, and twelve captions in French. S/he has to look at one of the pictures, choose the French which describes, it select the tile which has the same number and slot it into the appropriate place in the Stile tray. When all are assembled, the tiles form a pattern which tells him/her if his/her answers are correct or not. In order to see the result, the tray of tiles must be turned over and opened up with a flourish. This 'open sesame!' effect pleases younger learners very much, and the disappointment of seeing the wrong pattern gives them the motivation to try again. Whilst young beginners find the physical handling of the tiles and the tray satisfying, more experienced users are keen to compete with one another in races. (I have to admit I enjoy doing them myself.)

(6) 'Mini-flashcard Language Games' (see Chapter 12) are another invaluable source of reading, as well as speaking, practice which have sustained me over the years. There is nothing you cannot do with these games and players (of any age) love them. There are games with boards, dice, chance cards, counters etc. as well as the 'mini-flashcards' themselves, and photocopiable material to use for almost anything (although I personally never use these materials as a writing resource. I want the whole thing to remain 'just a game'). I try to hide the fact that they are a wonderful teaching resource by using them as treats for people who have worked hard, early finishers and so on. They can be used for any size group including individual or whole class. They can be used super-vised or unsupervised and in groups of same or mixed ability. Players (and teachers!) can make up different versions of the game or be as creative as they like. Start them off using a selection of cards most of which are familiar, and see their confidence grow. Groups of less advanced learners (with specially chosen cards relevant to them) offer an opportunity for everyone to win. There is only one major problem with these games, and that is getting them to stop!

(7) Of course there will be lots of reading material in your coursebook, and a big effort is made to make it both interesting and relevant. Use as much as you can, because it is the sort of thing which comes up in the GCSE exam. But young people tend to find anything from this source either dull or out-of-date or both. It is impossible to keep up with ever-changing youth culture (especially in view of the publishing time taken to launch a new course), and also to cater for the entire age range and level of sophistication of groups targeted. So that as much as one third of the reading items may be too sophisticated, and one third

too naive, for its audience. Or you may have to struggle with ancient books which your school has not replaced for years. Many schools are in this position, but if yours are pre-National Curriculum (!), you really are in a good position to get out the thumbscrews and use them on your head, co-ordinator, governors or anyone else who has access to the purse strings. If you are successful, however, do not throw away the old set in a moment of careless rapture. Every course has a few items which particularly suit some of your groups, and need not be consigned to oblivion, provided you have the storage space. I was once spotted (unfortunately) ransacking a room where all the school's ancient textbooks had been assembled, on the very morning some Tanzanians had arrived to take them away to be shipped to Tanzania! I was in search of a very successful treatment of French time, and a wonderful pictorial zodiac (my apologies to the Third World).

(8) Learners love crosswords, and books such as 'Le français par les mots croisés' from ELI[2] can be useful, although some of the vocabulary will inevitably be unfamiliar to your classes. So much easier to make your own, or have them made by pupils. (It is wise to provide younger ones with the grid. Making the grid can become the dominant theme of the whole exercise, and take as long as three weeks!) In this way your content is more relevant. Learners love to make any kind of puzzle for the rest of the class or a friend, as a writing exercise, which then becomes a reading test. They are never too young to start (see below), provided you check the finished product yourself. Photocopiable worksheet masters can be useful too, and I have enjoyed 'Fascinating Ideas for Flummoxed French Teachers'.[3] But make sure to keep these activities as a reward for those who have worked hard, or achieved something special for them (a category which all students have the option to fall into, or not, as they choose). If the whole class is instructed to make a crossword, it becomes 'work', and therefore 'boring' (generic word for 'undesirable').

(9) Students of all subjects suffer a surfeit of worksheets, and I endeavour to keep them to a minimum, but there is no doubt that they have a part to play. Besides practising both reading and writing skills, a good worksheet is essential for extra consolidation (the textbooks lack space to do this), for differentiation, for cover lessons, and for keeping a particularly noisy class quiet ('the stun-gun worksheet') (see Chapter 16).

(10) Much more fun than worksheets are the IT packages now available for modern languages. If your school has the facilities, from time to time have the whole class (or groups thereof), working on the new computers your school will by now be equipped with. As a complete computer illiterate and a slow starter, I managed over the years to master and use successfully with my classes three basic packages, starting with 'le Monde à Moi'.[4] This was an English language resource for slower learners converted into various languages, based on

pictures, and enabling children to learn from various visual games. It worked well and was very simple. More sophisticated, but not too sophisticated for me, was 'Pendown', or 'Pendown Etoiles'[5] as the newer version is called. This is a word processing package which enables students to produce news-letters, magazines, diaries, information sheets and all types of printed material in a stylish way. Users especially like the different fonts (one letter per page if required!), and the pictures. Whatever you have created, it looks infinitely better with a picture on it, or better still, at all four corners! (I wonder if British Telecom or the gas companies are aware of this?). 'Fun with Texts'[6] calls itself 'a multi-exercise authoring package', which seems to mean it has a lot of puzzles and games called things like 'Clozewrite', 'Scrambler' and 'Textsalad'. But don't let that worry you – that's the way they talk in IT. They can't help it. 'Gapkit', from the same company, seems to be a newer version ('Gap-filling and multiple-choice exercise authoring software') but with the addition of sound and pictures. I have not seen this, but it sounds highly desirable, and worth tracking down. Use these to produce exercises etc., tailored to suit your own groups exactly. Of course, the closer the connection between the vocabulary of the computer exercise or game, and the vocabulary of the course book, the more effective learning will be. It is important to make the two different kinds of work as compatible as possible. Provide any unfamiliar vocabulary for the average user, in order to maintain momentum. But let the high-flyers take their chance …

(11) The exciting new resource of IT will dazzle every member of your group. There are many reasons why they prefer to work with a computer rather than pen and paper:
  (a) mistakes are made in private;
  (b) mistakes don't matter: they can be instantly erased;
  (c) it is a more practical and physical way of working;
  (d) it involves no writing;
  (e) the learner can work at his own pace;
  (f) the computer doesn't care if the answer is right or wrong. It never comments and never gets impatient.
  (g) the slow reader or writer feels empowered;
  (h) most young people can use skills they already have;
  (i) computers are easier to use for groupwork;
  (j) the quality of the finished product is superior to anything which could be produced by hand.

(12) Having been a fearful and hesitant convert to IT in the classroom, I was really quite satisfied with what we were producing in all sorts of areas using these three packages. But just when I thought I had mastered the whole thing (!), and was giving myself a pat on the back, a new generation of software burst upon

the scene, infinitely more exciting, infinitely more sophisticated and having infinitely more potential. You will know which packages I am referring to because they all come in enormous boxes and have 'INTERACTIVE CD ROM' written on them (whatever that means). They also have wonderful visual effects, and soothing, enticing music, which really appeal to young people and to both of which they have become accustomed in the computer games they love. The most worrying thing, I thought, was that they also had 'automatic speech recognition'. (By this time I was quite pale.) Nevertheless, I decided to try them out. I remembered being exhorted in a government report, when IT first swept into schools, to 'show the same spirit of innovation that has transformed modern language teaching in the last twenty years', and decided it was my duty to be inspired. Once again. And inspired I was, to my surprise. My favourite, 'Tripleplus Play French',[7] has three levels of difficulty from age eight to adult, can speak to you, listen to your voice and give feedback on pronunciation, and has a record and play-back feature for conversation practice. You can see and experiment with a large selection of the latest software at CILT (Chapter 1) in Covent Garden, where the remarkably kindly and understanding staff are prepared to help you out no matter what you are searching for, or having difficulty with. Not only IT software, but everything is there: almost all recent teaching resources in existence. No language teacher can do without this haven. (Similar havens are provided at the Belfast and Stirling CILT, or visit the local Comenius centre in your region.)[8] I make it a rule never to buy anything in the IT area – usually at great expense – without trying it out first. You will know at once if it has the right flavour for your classes. It may be the latest and greatest thing of all time and still not suit your school. If you are lucky, your local teachers' centre may have an IT department which will help you find what you want, for example, putting material from your coursebook onto a disc for use in school (in the unlikely event that you can't do it yourself). If you have a restricted supply of machines, your class can still do useful IT work by taking turns (in very strict rotation). Pair-work or even groups of three are another alternative which enhance co-operative learning, but only if you keep a hawk's eye out for that scourge of IT – 'the one who does everything'! Be careful that this system doesn't degenerate into rewards for the elite computer buffs. Instead of giving them their turn with others, make them your 'disaster retrieval' team. The children who have no IT skills whatsoever are the ones who need to be using the machines (but they will not put themselves forward).

Stage 2: Working towards GCSE

(1) Long before Year 11, introduce the idea of reading a passage for formal comprehension. This means choosing a passage which will not necessarily be fun, nor even interesting. Begin with short passages and a few questions in

English, and pass onto longer and longer ones, still with English questions. There is lots of suitable material for comprehension in your average coursebook. Jot a few questions suited to the class on the board and leave them to it. For early finishers you are confident have done well, put up a few more difficult ones, making them up as you go along, as though you had not anticipated this turn of events. Perhaps giving a choice of doing three out of five. If you give a choice, they will probably do them all anyway, just to show how you have underestimated them. Nothing pleases the high-flyers more than to think they have exceeded your expectations.

(2) Your classes will all have seen letters written by French penfriends etc. in your collection of realia, but now is the time to draw their attention to the fact that some of the items they may have to deal with in the exam will be in French handwriting, adult or child. (Those of your students who have done an exchange, or have a French penfriend, will have an advantage here). Concentrate their minds on the examples available to them in textbooks (ancient courses might provide additional practice), and also make a collection of the real thing, give them one each and leave them to make what they can of it.

(2) Starting in Year 10 and for the whole of Year 11 follow as far as possible the exact format of the exam according to your board, using as many actual past papers as you can lay your hands on. Past papers are the most valuable teaching aid you can supply at this stage. If your department has none and cannot afford them, make an appeal to the PTA, the local independent school, or anybody! It is even worth buying them yourself and photocopying them at school. For every paper they will have to sit, in order to reduce exam nerves learners need to know exactly what awaits them, how it is set out, how many questions there are likely to be (and how difficult or easy), what number of pages (many marks are lost as a result of turning over two pages together), exactly what kind of questions will be asked in which language, and most importantly, how long the whole thing will last.

(3) Panic often leads to a headlong rush at the passage, and a headlong dive into hectic word-for-word translation. Explain that as the excerpt will probably be quite long, this is not a good idea, because what the candidate will hand in when time is up will be only a quarter, if that, of the questions, answered very badly.

(4) Some sort of 'training' (thumbscrews?) must take place to ensure that they read the instructions and questions *first* (very hard to do), and only then proceed to a quick reading of the passage to pick up what they can. It is important to be aware of what the questions are before first tackling the piece, because:

    (a) You hopefully get an idea of what it is all about from the nature of the questions themselves.

    (b) You may notice in what part of the passage the answers to the questions are likely to be found. Remember that they are usually asked in the order in which the answers appear in the text.

(c) You may spot some of the actual answers.

(d) You may realise the meaning of one of the questions you just did not understand on the first reading.

(5) Reading the questions first is a skill some candidates find almost impossible to acquire (the impatient ones, plus the ones in total panic!) Use your Gestapo skills on the whole class. *No-one* reads the passage until they have proved that they know what the questions are. Test them. People will be surprisingly deceitful about this. They will peep. If you have trouble, you may have to put the questions only on the OHP and work with them, before you give out the passage itself. 'Can this be?', you ask yourself. Yes, I'm afraid it can. When it comes to exam technique, human nature, as in many areas of life, will often overwhelm good sense. Your insistence, plus lots of repetition, are the only hope that good sense will prevail.

(6) Impress the following on them in any way you can. Make them repeat after you: *First answer what questions you can*. How much easier this will be without the presence of that double-edged sword, the dictionary. Candidates found it so difficult to accept and resign themselves to the fact there would not be time to look up all the words. There were even candidates who liked to look up the words that they knew, (just to make sure!).

(7) Do not answer the questions in strict order, spending longer on the ones you can't do. This is quite a popular technique, but time will run out long before you reach the end, and you will not have answered easy questions further on in the text for which you could have gained marks. Answer all the questions you can first. Only when you have done that, start on those you cannot. Find the sentences you think may contain the answer you need. Work only on the questions you are confident you have understood. Leave the others until last.

(8) Deal last of all with any question you did not understand. Now that you are more familiar with the text, you may find you can work it out after all. If you have made no progress towards doing so, use your knowledge of the rest of the passage to think of what sort of question *might* be asked, and answer it. You have nothing to lose by guessing, and you just might be right!

(9) Do not panic if there are many long words in the passage which you do not understand. You are not supposed to. When you are abroad, you can never understand *every word* that is spoken to you in the foreign language. Even your teacher cannot(!). What you must be able to do is to pick out the information you need. This is the skill which you are expected to use in this paper. It has always been vital, and is part of the reason use of the dictionary has been abandoned. Students would begin feverishly looking up all the difficult new words, never got to the end of the paper and lost many marks.

(10) Candidates entered for the higher paper will have to cope with much more material which is unfamiliar to them, including tenses they have never used, more authentic extracts from newspapers etc., extracts from fiction, more advanced letters, and advertisements. Some of the material will contain messages which are not 'explicit', or definitely stated, and you will have to work out what they mean. It is not a question of finding the exact words in the text which state the answer. You have to guess what you think is appropriate. For instance, if you read 'Après avoir fini ses études, Florence avait l'intention de se marier aussitôt que possible. Elle attendait avec impatience le moment où elle allait partir de chez elle, de ses trois petits frères et de sa mère infirme', you might be asked why Florence wanted to marry. The answer is not clearly stated, in the text, but you might deduce that she was unhappy at home.

(11) For those who have time to use them, I have seen some very interesting IT revision packages for GCSE. High-flyers needing extra stimulation can benefit from working on one of these, but for the average candidate, time may be better spent mastering the material they have learnt so far really thoroughly. Unfamiliar additions to their repertoire, (and there are bound to be some), could be confusing at this late stage.

Fun activity for reading: 'le journal'

The most successful reading text I ever created was a school newspaper. Everyone loves reading about themselves, even in a foreign language. Because the name of the school was 'Silver Jubilee', for the sake of alliteration I called it 'le Journal de Jubilee', and because it was a middle school for nine to 13-year-olds, it had to have lots of pictures, cartoons etc. Depending on the age-group, you can include almost any-thing, and have contributions by your pupils etc., but I think the most important thing about such a newspaper is that nothing should go in that is not either interesting to the school community, or entertaining.

Interesting

Finding topical items to write about was not a problem (I only did one per year!), and a lot happens in a school during that time. You can include any school happening of interest to the pupils, such as:

(1) General results: sports results, merit badges, prizes won etc.

(2) School events, particularly the school trip to Boulogne, plus (less prominently!), the safari park, the activity holiday and the rest. Not forgetting a big spread for the French play. Use cartoons and pictures to make these events interesting – straight narrative is not enough ('boring').

(3) Advertisements for the school fair, French fashion show, bingo etc., with illustration as above.

(4)	Appropriate staff news, i.e. something you know the children are interested in e.g. an impending happy event for a popular young member of staff, or the arrival of a new librarian. (I did say appropriate.)

(5)	Local news of interest to the school. Unfortunately not much happened in our area, and all I ever managed was a piece after the Gulf War about the brothers and ex-pupils who had gone to fight. I hope you work nearer to the hub of things. (After I left, the school had a visit from the Queen!)

Entertaining

Intersperse the text with anything you can find which will amuse your audience, as long as you can provide a French caption for it. (If, like me, 'interspersing text' is not one of your talents, get one of your computer whiz-kids to do it for you.) It is easy to find suitable pictures and cartoons – provided you have access to mountains of very ancient textbooks – and you can copy suitable headings and headlines from French magazines. You can be as creative as you like here, and also include items from your pupils, but because of the short time at my disposal I was restricted to:

(1)	Original French cartoons which seemed accessible, or almost accessible, to the age group.

(2)	Any cartoons which could be supplied with a caption making them relevant to the audience, e.g. characters looking like members of staff, or children.

(3)	Competitions: guess the dinner lady, guess the weight etc. of the new arrival, a quiz about France (in English), spot the difference. (Although no-one ever actually entered any of them. I never found out why not.)

(4)	Partly accessible extracts from French magazines about English pop music or films.

Try to have something for *everyone* in your newspaper (e.g. the quiz in English and 'le jeu des vingt erreurs'), use the talents you find in your classes, and it will be fun to read for the pupils and fun for you to do.

Notes to Chapter 15

1.	'Stile French', Thomas Nelson, Freepost, ITPS Ltd. North Way, Andover, Hants, SP10.
2.	'Le français par les mots croisés', European Language Institute, US (ISBN 888514814).
3.	'Fascinating Ideas for Flummoxed French Teachers', HarperCollins Publishers, Westerhill Road, Bishopbriggs, Glasgow G64 1BR.
4.	'Le Monde à Moi', Semerc, Granada Learning Ltd, Quay Street, Manchester, M60 9EA. (Now available for Acorn only).
5.	'Pendown etoiles', Logotron, Longman Group Ltd, Harlow, Essex, CM20 2JE.
6.	'Fun with Texts', Camsoft, 10, Wheatfield Close, Maidenhead, Berks, SL6 3PS.
7.	'Tripleplay Plus French', Syracuse Language Systems Inc., distributed by Potential Software, Treloar Farm, Wendron, Helston, Cornwall, TR13 0NL.
8.	There is a Comenius Centre near you: Sunderland, Lancaster, York, Leeds, Blackburn, Manchester, Bangor, Leicester, Birmingham, Cambridge, Oxford, Bristol,Truro, Exeter, Southampton, West Sussex.

Chapter 16
The four skills: writing

Q Why is writing so stressful?

Q What can be done to make it easy?

Q How can candidates take advantage of the degree of freedom offered in tasks set on this paper?

Q Will they manage without the dictionary?

Q What is 'trawling'?

Q Is learners' ability to check their own work an impossible dream?

Q Is there an easy way to reach a higher grade?

Q Why worksheets?

A Because it requires more complex memorisation and attention to detail than the other three skills

A Nothing: accept it as arduous, and work on detailed memorisation of basic material over a long period

A Candidates can learn to make use of the choice they are offered by selecting only from the store of vocabulary they have memorised

A Certainly: a dictionary can be a snare and a delusion, a waster of vital time and an invitation to inaccuracy

A 'Trawling' is learning how to separate what you do know from what you don't

A Yes, unless they can memorise (and use) a concrete framework to follow

A Yes, by using more complex language following the twelve tips below

A Worksheets are an essential aid to consolidation and differentiation, because they can be tailored to suit your individual class, used for cover lessons and, in extremis, for disciplinary purposes. They can go where no coursebook has gone before!

Stage 1: The most difficult skill of all?

(1) Writing is often thought of as the most difficult of the four skills. It can remain a problem long after the others have become familiar. Learners have difficulty in improving their performance, and are not sure how to do so. This is not really surprising. Think of it like this: in order to achieve a good grade in the writing papers, two distinct abilities are required, which are much less important in speaking, reading and listening. And they are:
   (a) attention to detail;
   (b) good spelling.

(2) These are skills which some people naturally have (lucky them). If you are learning a foreign language and you do not actually possess these abilities in English, you are unlikely to display them in any other language. Students should not tear their hair out if writing in French seems much harder than everything else. More effort will be needed in order to achieve the higher grades, but it can be done. Foundation level was devised to help these candidates, and they can certainly succeed here, but it would be a pity if poor writing skills were to bar an otherwise good candidate from a higher grade. What can they do about it? Memorisation of a small amount of material, and constant repetition, is the only option, I'm afraid. Writing does not come naturally: it has to be programmed in little by little, in the smallest detail.

(3) As a teacher, you cannot afford to start this training from the beginning. Be flexible in the first few years. Have only fun writing activities. Use puzzles, crosswords, mots mystères, etc. made by the class where possible, with not too much emphasis on spelling, or grammatical points (with the exception of display work or anything going home). Worksheets can be fun at many levels. Do not create anxiety by setting high standards for writing too soon. This is one of the main factors contributing to the famous 'I can't do French!' syndrome.

(4) After the first few years, given an 'average' mixed ability class (if there is such a thing), make your own assessment, which will depend on what time you have available to you, and on the progress of the group so far. If you are a middle school you will have to liaise with the school(s) at which your pupils will be taking the final exam, and negotiate their natural desire for the children you are sending to have made good progress in accurate writing, with your desire to keep their interest and motivation alive. After all, this must be the most effective approach to exam success in the end. Bear in mind that if you are unfortunate enough to work with an upper school which expects your pupils to arrive there with writing of almost GCSE standard (and some do), you could perhaps ask them what they propose doing for the next three years …?

(5) When you feel a start should be made on more accurate writing, make it a success situation for all by starting with copy-writing. If you start writing for accuracy of any sort, and especially creative writing, too early, confidence will be damaged. Your first tasks must be accessible to everyone, which means they must be very short (!), and using material which is completely familiar to all. They have to feel: 'Yes, I can do this!' An imaginary postcard of just a few words, to a friend in France might be a good starting point. If the school day trip to Boulogne is within living memory, a fun postcard to family or friends would be equally brief and be more relevant, both to those who went and to those who did not. (Children like to send a card home, on an 'I woz here!' basis. Does it matter if you return home long before your carrier pigeon?) Whatever the early writing, make sure it is a meaningful activity, in other words, one

which they can imagine performing in real life. You might choose to project two possible postcards on the OHP, and ask the class to translate them.

(6) When translated (they should be too easy to call for a proper translation competition), ask the class to choose which one they are going to learn. The task is always more motivating if you allow them a choice. A vote must be taken because only one of the two can be used. Before you start, give a lecture on the enormity of the task before them. Emphasise the importance and difficulty of what they have to do, in order to dispel the impression they may have, as many do when writing in English, that writing 'just comes out', right or wrong, and there's not a lot to be done about it. Make it clear that a lot *can* be done about it, and that they are going to do it. Starting now!

(7) Make a clear space round writing in French, explaining that it is nothing to do with writing in English, and is a special technique which they are going to learn. In this way you are helping the anxieties of those who have difficulties in English. Point out a few salient points there might be on the card, such as accents (of which there must not be many), and ask them how many people in the class they think can copy out the postcard without any mistakes, including the 'salient points'. The number who succeed may be surprisingly many, or surprisingly few, but continue with this game until almost all have made a perfect copy (this is why it has to be such a very short postcard). Make it out of card, looking as much like an actual postcard as possible. They then take their final and correct copy home to practice making a copy for homework. Half or less will do, depending on the progress made in class. Before the finished product goes home, let those who have still not achieved perfection feel that they have made substantial progress, and make any corrections yourself if necessary. Next lesson repeat the process of copy-writing once, before an attempt is made to copy from memory. Congratulate all who have *improved*, whether they have successfully reproduced the few lines from memory or not. If you have not already done so, teach them how to mark each other's work, noting the number of mistakes at the end. (The process can only work with self-marking, otherwise the whole thing becomes unwieldy and time-consuming). This note is very important and the object of the whole exercise: it is their target for improvement next time.

(8) Continue to repeat this method, gradually introducing new cards and increasing the difficulty of the material to suit the group. After a certain number of attempts on the first card, do not expect that all the learners will have succeeded. Pass on to a new piece and go back to revise the original in later weeks. Returning to original work is essential, because this kind of precise learning grows incrementally with each piece of writing they attempt. Progress will occur very slowly for those with substantial difficulties. So at all costs avoid early failure and discouragement by

making sure you do not require 'perfection', but effort and improvement, so that all can succeed according to their abilities.

(9) Young people have strange ideas about the learning of 'spellings'. Play team games with the spelling of words from 'j'aime' and 'cartes postales' to 'amities' and 'bienvenue' (team games so that even the weakest spellers can take part. They may not be able to spell them but they will have an emotional investment in seeing them spelt correctly). Don't forget to teach a simple 'read, cover, write, check' technique for learning the spelling of new words. Never assume that they know it. It is surprising how many seem to forget this technique, which is essential for success. Disabuse them gently of the idea that good spelling just happens, or can be acquired as a result of either reading words over and over again, or staring intently at them *for a very long time.*

(10) Successful progress must be within the grasp of everyone, and the only desired outcome at this stage. Do not worry about the monotony of this system. If they copy and learn nothing but material which will appear in their writing exam paper, you are focusing their effort where it is most needed, simplifying their task, and equipping them with a priceless store which they can draw on almost effortlessly when the time comes. If a topic you had not anticipated should appear, they will always be able to draw on some part of their accurate fund of written material, which has been thoroughly *memorised.*

Stage 2: Working towards GCSE

(1) Familiarity with the GCSE paper must start at the latest in Year 10. As with all the papers, candidates must be aware of the number of questions, the time available for each, the different sections, which to attempt, and so on. The format of all likely questions, which may be in English or French, must be memorised. Failure to properly understand the question is an unnecessary way to lose marks. To increase confidence, let them make a list at the very beginning of Year 10 of what they will need to be able to write at Foundation level. Typically, that will be:

(a) A short list of individual words or short phrases, for example, what to take on a picnic. (Grade F–G)

(b) A 30–40 word message (approximately five tasks) in the present tense. (D–G)

(c) An 80–90 word letter including past and future tenses and your own opinions. (C–D)

(2) If you are a candidate and that list seems to you to be a giant memory overload, even over two years, be encouraged by one important fact: in writing, as in no other part of the exam, you have quite a bit of freedom as to *what* you write. You have more choice than in any other paper. Some boards give you a choice of actual task (EDEXCEL, MEG, WJEC, SEG), but most do not. The choice you

have with all boards however, lies in what language you use. If you are asked to write a list of things you might take with you on a picnic, or for a stay in hospital, for example, you will not be obliged to write any particular word at all. If you cannot remember the French for 'hamper', or 'hairbrush', it will not matter in the least, because you will be free to write something else, anything else, as long as it is appropriate. (I'm assuming that you will be well-prepared with basic vocabulary.) Most important of all, you will not need to waste a moment looking up words in the dictionary. Especially words like these, which are not easy. For letters and accounts, you will by now have memorised a few stock phrases to suit any situation. After all, if you have to write that hardy perennial, a postcard/letter about your summer holidays, the sky's the limit. (There's nothing you can't get up to on a summer holiday …)

(3) You can only benefit from this wonderful freedom, however, if you learn to distinguish between what you don't know and what you do know, ignoring the former and using strictly only what you *do* know. This is harder than it sounds. Some candidates used to find it impossible to let go of the idea they first thought of. They could not resist looking up 'hamper' in the dictionary. They had to be trained, threatened, bribed, begged or bullied into giving up this commendable, but dangerous, little habit. You are fortunate, you will not have that temptation. In all cases, if you have a choice of what to say, say something that you have *memorised*.

(4) For example, if you are telling a story illustrated by pictures, as you often are, be careful not to be mesmerised by the huge drawing of a boat. You are not asked to comment on every single item in the picture (if you did you would be way over the word limit). You should know exactly how many words you need to write per picture and check that you do so. Writing more will not result in more marks, the unwanted words will simply be ignored. Less simply, they will have wasted valuable time needed for other questions. Some candidates feel obliged to mention the boat, whether they know what the French is or not. Using the word 'boat' is not the object of the exercise. Saying something intelligent about the picture is. You will have memorised at some stage a phrase such as 'nous avons passé les vacances en France', or 'il a fait bon voyage', either of which will be better received (because correct), than some bungled version of your means of transport

(5) A total ban must be imposed on translating from English into French. When confronted by unfamiliar material, learners like to think that word for word translation from English might just do it. Of course it never does. Gestapo tactics will be needed again to convince some students not to do this. Give them lots of examples of the pitfalls, and lots of practise in trawling through what they have memorised so far in order to find something suitable to use. This is a process which does not come naturally to young learners. They find it

difficult and tend to avoid it. It is a skill which each individual must learn for himself, often with special help from the teacher. The memory bank must not simply be there, it must be accessible at a moment's notice. A thorough trawl can only be accomplished after at least one year's intensive work on memorisation and regular repetition of the material.

(6) Making a fair copy of your finished work is usually a waste of time and effort. It can also involve the making of entirely new mistakes. For every fault found and corrected, another may creep in and remain unnoticed. It is unfortunately a fact, most inconvenient for teachers of foreign languages, that learners find 'checking' their own work next to impossible. It is hard to say why. They are excellent at checking the work of their peers, and should have had lots of practice at this from the first year. But they do need a concrete visual stimulus to refer to, which of course is not possible in the exam situation. The nearest alternative is to give them a checklist which they have learnt until they dream about it. It must be short enough to write out at the start of the paper in just a few seconds. If it is laborious, they will not do it. (Preparatory plans in all subjects mostly go by the board in the heat of the moment. Exam panic rules, and the great fear of 'not finishing in time!' takes over.) The list could be something like this:

(a) question?	or even:	qu.
(b) tense?		T.
(c) avoir/être?		Av/et
(d) past part.?		P.p.
(e) agree?		Agr.
(f) accents?		Acc.
(g) past/fut.?		P/fut.
(h) mon avis?		av.

(7) As with listening, help will have to be given with the very strong visual element in these papers. Some people find the sequence and meaning of graphics more obvious than others. Practice is the only answer. Don't be afraid of 'gender bias'. The fact is that boys tend to be better at deciphering these tasks than girls, just as girls are better at performing others. Modern language teachers should not be afraid to discriminate, however 'politically incorrect' it may seem. When learning languages, boys on the whole will need a much bigger carrot, in terms of variety, competition, excitement, achievement, and recognition, than girls if they are not to switch off. In modern language learning, it is unfortunately true, and has been shown by much research, that there are real differences of boredom threshold and persistence between the sexes.[1] Don't overlook them.

(8) In the stress of the exam situation, students often leave out parts of tasks because of the pressure they put themselves under to finish. They leap ahead,

and fail to notice part of the instructions they are given, or forget them as they rush from one to another at breakneck speed. Total familiarity with the paper, and type of question, can help with this, but part of the first item on their checklist: 'question', should be to make sure that:

(a) they have understood the question, and

(b) they have answered all its parts.

(9)   Using the past, present and future tenses will be essential for a good grade, but need not be intimidating if a sufficient number of verbs in the three tenses have been memorised. By 'sufficient', I mean enough to cover a variety of predictable situations. There should be no tension about forming the appropriate tense from scratch in the heat of battle, it should be already there waiting to be used. Remember for the future tense that the use of 'aller' with the infinitive is acceptable at Foundation level.

Stage 3: obtaining a higher grade

(1)   So you want to obtain a grade A*–B? All you have to do is what you have already done at Foundation level, plus a 100– 150 word letter or article. The idea of this is to give you scope for:

(a) more complex language;

(b) longer and more detailed descriptions or accounts.

(2)   An article is more or less the same as a letter, without the headings, but in some ways it is more difficult. It is more focused and usually has fewer topics than a letter. In a letter you can range wide with your choice of language, but in an article you must address its subject, whatever it may be, from start to finish. Keep this in mind if you have a choice. The same applies to the presentation, if your board requires one. If you find yourself having a problem with monotony in an article or presentation, try to change the pronoun from time to time e.g. 'je suis allé' to 'nous sommes allés'. If the future tense seems hard to place, use it at the end as a future intention e.g. 'j'irai voir les Alpes l'année prochaine parce que …'

(3)   Include as many different tenses as you can: the present, perfect, imperfect, future, and conditional as a minimum. Avoid the use of 'aller' plus infinitive until you have proved your overall knowledge of the future tense. This may sound intimidating, but all you have to do is make yourself a short list of two all-purpose phrases for each of these tenses which can be used in any context, and learn it.

(4)   Do not be afraid to use language from the instructions you are given on the paper. It is there to help you.

(5)   Write longer sentences joined together by words such as 'qui, que, donc, puis, alors, mais, car, parce que'.

(6)   Learn a handy little list of all-purpose phrases which will make your writing

more complex, such as 'd'abord, ensuite, soudain, après cela, enfin, quand, (mal)heureusement'.

(7) Use a variety of easy-to-use verbal phrases such as 'arrivé à la plage, après avoir, avant de, j'ai décidé de, il a commencé à'.

(8) Learn a description of personal emotion to suit any situation so that you will never be lost for words (étonné, triste, surpris, fâché, content, malheureux, deçu, furieux, bouleversé, terrifié'!).

(9) Vary the ways in which you express your opinions ('il me semble que, je crois que, à mon avis, j'ai toujours pensé que' etc.).

(10) Include as many details as you can (adjectives, adverbs, description and explanation).

(11) Time phrases can be used in any context and create a good impression ('à la fin de la journée, pendant ce temps, après cela, cinq minutes plus tard').

(12) Use pronouns to avoid repetition ('je l'ai laissé', 'il m'a vu', 'on nous a donné').

Fun activities for writing
Liaison between schools

Devising and sending attractive display work to other schools can be fun. If you are in a middle school, send up display work by your Year 8, which they will be delighted to see on view when they arrive at upper school next year. If you are in an upper school, your feeder school(s) will appreciate even more items sent by you for them to display. They will be particularly impressed if the material is in a variety of languages, and this will be good for the prestige of modern languages in general, as well as turning thoughts towards new opportunities ahead. Be sure that what is sent, however, in either direction, is intrinsically appealing, and does not consist of dull pieces of original writing copied from the exercise book etc. This will only be a fun activity if there is lots of freedom to compose and copy at will, using any material which takes their fancy and which will be entertaining to the recipients.

French penfriends

The same rule must apply to the 'letter to the French penfriend' project, which so often bites the dust after the first solemn and painstaking letter constructed out of blood, sweat and tears. Starting so optimistically, this enterprise often founders after one, or at most two letters. Is it because the writer (both writers?) feel restricted to their narrow repertoire of foreign language, in which real communication is not likely to take place? Correspondents should feel able to communicate in whichever language suits what they have to say, and send any material they can find (poster, photo, article, drawings, cartoons, advertisement, tapes etc.) which either interests or entertains them or their friend.

Greeting cards

Younger learners enjoy making cards for various events to take home to their families and friends. They particularly like to be the only person in the class taking home a card for a special event such as the birth of a new baby. This is so much more special than making a Christmas card along with the rest of the class, although this too has its attractions – especially if there is a prize for the best one (Mars bar again?). Have Christmas or Easter cards ready well before the event, because the best ones make a wonderful display for the front corridor before they go home!

Worksheets

As every pupil will tell you, worksheets can be very, very boring. It is in their nature to be so. In some schools, whether for reasons of finance or policy, they form the inevitable basis of every lesson, and quickly lose the freshness of a change of medium. Do your best to make them palatable, because they do have a part to play, as I was reluctantly forced to concede at an early stage in my teaching career. This is your opportunity to really tailor your material to suit your classes, and enjoy having a perfect fit between their ability and the task before them. Nothing gives a class more satisfaction.

The recent trend towards using target language only for instruction and explanation has made coursebooks an infinitely more confusing and less homely place for an average learner to be. Looking at a typical page, a class will have no idea of what is to be done for each exercise, diminishing their feeling that they can cope alone. Extensive teacher input is required. Very long units are also a bad idea. A 20-page unit on 'school life' is too great a burden for the average learner. Classes become bored with the subject. Not to mention being discouraged by the size of the task. Worst of all, the end is never in sight! When they finally limp through to the final summary of what they are supposed to have 'learnt', they are exhausted and depressed. They may even feel that they have forgotten most of it.

You can use worksheets to break up 'monster' units and give empowerment to the student. Divide them up into suitable sections and provide a worksheet with all the material they will need (plus a translation), and treat them as totally separate teaching 'modules', with suitable celebration and satisfaction for teacher and taught at the end of each. Then if at all feasible, move on to something new on a different topic. Come back to 'school life' later. In this way you hope to keep your class interested.

Long ago in the mists of time, my average-to-low ability classes moved on from Michael Buckby's 'Action' (panic at the advent of the National Curriculum!) to more modern coursebooks. They greatly missed the useful first section for each unit which laid out clearly, with translation, the basic material to be used. Not just the new material, but other vital items, as a reminder of what they should know as well as what they were about to learn. In French and English. The great usefulness of this page did not strike me until we had been working for several months with a more exciting course. The new books were more up to date, more attractive, more entertaining, more relevant and more varied. Why were they harder to use with these pupils? After some thought, I came to the conclusion that these learners needed:

(1)   to see from the beginning exactly what they have to learn;
(2)   to see it in English as well as the target language in order to remove the stress of 'not knowing';
(3)   to feel that they can digest (or 'get their head round'?) what is required;
(4)   to feel secure in the knowledge that they have something to refer back to at any time.

   The opening page in 'Action' gave a feeling of security and confidence that they could cope, especially because of the use of English. In the interests of TL use for coursebook instruction, a list of new material will often only appear in French, obviously of little use the class until they have actually finished learning it. The feeling of mastery is lost if there is no indication of what is to come, and as they flounder on through a maze of unfamiliar language, particularly if the unit is long. Knowing where to find everything they need enables independent learning. If your course does not offer this, for certain classes you can supply it by providing a worksheet with all the material they will need for the current unit. Whatever the textbook cannot do, you need to do with a worksheet. They are useful for:

(1)   consolidation;
(2)   differentiation;
(3)   cover lessons;
(4)   keeping a noisy class quiet ('the stun-gun worksheet').

   To be successful for the above purposes each of these work-sheets will be slightly different.

(1)   *Consolidation.* Textbooks have a space problem. They are very expensive to produce, and cannot provide sufficient consolidation for every topic. You, on the other hand, are free to go on and on with the same point as long as you (and they), can stand it. Don't be afraid to include far more repetition than you might think bearable. Mixed ability learners enjoy repetition. They do not find it as tedious as you do.
(2)   *Differentiation.* Include many sections of increasing difficulty, carefully designed so that only the high-flyers get to the end. This is better than giving out two worksheets, which will instantly be called 'hard' and 'easy peasy' (the latter being heartily despised and only done by failures!). Make it very difficult

for anyone, however hard-working, to finish. You could end a worksheet on the topic of school, for example, with a section 8 consisting of 'Fais un plan de ton école. Marque les pieces en français'. (!) The longer the worksheet, the more the high-flyers will struggle to be the first to finish. A worksheet which does not challenge these learners in particular, does not engage them, and also results in organisational scrappiness as some members of the class dispose of them in two minutes each.

(3) *Cover lessons*. This worksheet must be completely free-standing. All the information needed should be at hand in the textbook or elsewhere, and your colleagues will appreciate the fact that they are not required to answer enquiries about the work during the lesson. Make sure they are aware of this before they arrive. Pupils are sophisticated about teacher weakness for explanation (we sometimes become addicted to it), and see taking advantage of the innocent as an excellent way to while away the lesson, and *avoid doing the work*! The cover worksheet should also have a more limited variety of activities than the normal worksheet: forget small conversation sections and pairwork, if you want to remain friends with colleagues covering for you. Be sure to have one ready for Christmas. But it can be less draconien than:

(4) *'The stun-gun worksheet'*. There is nothing like a carefully planned worksheet for keeping a class quiet. By their nature, textbooks have to be divided into too many short sections, and have too much variety, to make for unbroken and concentrated writing. The 'stun-gun' worksheet' can provide just that. I once started work in a school where there were Year 8 classes who were accustomed to rioting during French lessons. They had had a succession of temporary teachers and teachers who knew no French, and saw no reason why my arrival should make any difference. They continued to maintain their tradition. After a couple of lessons and the beginnings of laryngitis, I decided that I would give up my objective of teaching, and aim instead at 'keeping them quiet'. It seemed a sensible first step. To this end I constructed a 'stun-gun worksheet', the characteristics of which are:

- It must be very, very easy.
- It is completely free-standing. No-one has to come out and ask *anything* at any time. Instructions must be in *English*.
- It is based strictly on whatever unit of the coursebook the class is 'on' (i.e. supposed to be studying). All the information they need must be there to be copied or looked up. There must be no question of dictionaries (euphemism for scuffles in the corner).
- It must have very many sections, all slightly different, so that the reluctant feel that they are having a constant change of activity, and making never-ending progress from section to section. But in practice they must be restricted entirely

to two skills: reading and writing. Forget the drawing sections (diversion tactics are innumerable here, starting with the well-known 'borrowing a ruler'). And forget the little role-play at the end – far too disruptive. Any activity other than reading and writing will be too much of an interruption to the fragile peace and quiet you have managed to establish.

- It must take place in total silence. Lulled into a false sense of security by what has happened (can it be peace?), you may feel tempted to leave your 'hypnotic stare at the front of the room' pose (always unwise in these circumstances), and patrol round looking at work and giving words of praise. Most teachers suffer from this compulsion, but you must fight against it. Do not give in. You are right, they may respond well to some feedback, but alternatively they may use it as an excuse to riot. In a troubled class unused to good management, any kindly impulse on the part of staff may be seen as a sign of weakness. In this particular school, children seemed able to work only in total silence (not an ideal situation for a teacher of modern languages). Never disturb this sort of class for any reason. There is quite a technique to this. Some teachers cannot manage it at all. (Remaining silent for any time at all is out of the question for some, and a severe strain for most of us). But keeping quiet is not the whole of it. There must be no action of any sort from you. Literally. Do not blow your nose, do not leave your seat, do not open a window, do not look in your bag, above all, do not speak to anyone. (If you feel you may be having a heart attack, do so quietly on the floor where they can't see you.)

- It must never, never be finished. I learnt during student struggles to bring education and discipline to the unruly, that the really important thing about a good work-sheet for this purpose, and the reason you had to create your own, was not that it should be relevant to their experience, attractive, differentiated, enjoyable or even educational, but that no-one could ever finish it. This kind of class can only concentrate if everyone else is concentrating. Whatever the early finisher is doing, it will distract every single person in the room, and be an excuse for the end of work as they know it!

- Start a new sheet each lesson, however little has been done on the original. A fresh sheet will give them fresh motivation. Starting a new one will engage their attention, and be seen as an opportunity to perhaps do better than they did before. Finishing anything off from a previous lesson is anathema to this type of class.

- After some time my reputation as a 'good teacher' in the eyes of Year 8 was established, and I was able to begin to teach. But only gradually …

Note to Chapter 16

1. Clark, A. (1993) *Gender on the Agenda*. London: CILT.

6¹¹ en classe

A VENIR

Après les vacances de Paques TROIS professeurs nouveaux arriveront à Silver Jubilee! Mademoiselle Harper (en ce moment prof à l'école de Goldington), Monsieur Bowden, prof d'anglais, qui vient de Milton Keynes, et Madame Dickson (en ce moment professeur à l'école de St. Bede). SURPRISE quand elle a rendu visite a 7⁹, 6¹² et 6¹³ la semaine dernière. Elle aidera Mme Pleuger dans la salle 7. BIENVENUE à Mlle Thomas, prof de maths et à Mme Horler qui prend charge de la bibliothèque. Son livre préféré c'est *Lord of The Rings* de Tolkien.

Chapter 17

The sound of music

Q How enthusiastic are learners about songs in the target language?
Q What do I do if I can't sing?
Q How can I make a success of public performances?
Q Why are songs helpful for language learning?
Q What if most of the songs are too difficult for my classes?
A As enthusiastic as you are, as long as you choose songs they can relate to
A They won't mind, and there's always the tape back-up
A By controlling 'H.E.T.S.' stress and forward planning
A Because using music, movement and emotion stimulates the affective and creative area of the brain, improves short-term memory and enhances the important sense of mastery
A Preparation by translation, several listenings and practice of problem pronunciation before the first attempt is the answer. Or have them sing selected verses/lines only.

With a song in my heart

From the moment I set foot in France I fell in love with French popular music. At 13, dancing to records was raging amongst my exchange partner's friends, and during the hot afternoons, in the mountain village near Carcassonne, we would gather at someone's house to dance to records. Every house had a large cool basement perfect for the purpose. There was 'pop' music, some of it in English, but also some of the French classics. I fell in love to 'Marjolaine', had my heart broken to 'Sur ma vie', and said sad goodbyes to 'Les feuilles mortes'. All over Europe, exchange partners at this impressionable age were probably doing the same thing.

The joy of singing like Piaf (sort of)

But listening was not enough. For some reason I had an overpowering urge to *learn the words*. When I came home I spent hours listening and scribbling, pondering over the more obscure bits, determined to commit the whole thing to memory. Why? Why are songs important to us? Who knows, but they are. And of course, from the language point of view, they led to mastery, complete mastery. Here was something which could be learnt and sung just like a native. When I sang, my pronunciation was perfect, my halting spoken French quite forgotten. For that brief moment I became the speaker of beautiful French that I longed to be. As I grew up, Trenet, Piaf, Aznavour, Brel etc. came into the picture, and were a lasting source of pleasure. And at the other end of the scale, at university, I enjoyed a group in which students who had worked in 'colonies de vacances' for the summer, shared their repertoire of childrens' songs.

Don't worry if you can't sing

Embarking on a career in teaching, I had no expectation that my own enthusiasm could be passed on to my classes. I saw my passion as a private thing, of no interest to children beyond one or two nursery songs for beginners. I knew this was the case because of one vital impediment: I couldn't sing in tune to save my life. Tape was not an option in those far-off days. (I often wonder how we managed to teach modern languages at all.) How could I possibly stand in front of thirty pupils and croak? When 'Frère Jacques' appeared in the first textbook, I decided to ignore it. But something must have driven me to try, and the class loved it. Don't worry in the least if you can't sing, it doesn't seem to matter. The children sympathise. They enjoy being able to do it so much better.

Pity those who croak

Don't be afraid to start with a tape back-up, to give the necessary confidence. But be careful that the recording you choose is at the correct pitch for your learners. Many commercial tapes are pitched too high, and no-one will be able to reach the high notes (including yourself), or enjoy singing them. One of the advantages of singing yourself is that you can vary the range to suit the class. Or yourself. There must be a thousand different recordings of a song like 'Au clair de la lune', but you can only find the right songs for you and your classes by *listening to them first*. This may involve visits to CILT (Chapter 1), poking around record shops, listening to other peoples' tapes, listening to everything you come across, recording from radio, recording in France especially, and generally scavenging as a way of life. This may turn out to continue over quite a long period, perhaps as much as twenty years! I never did find a recording of some of the Christmas songs which suited my classes, and everyone had to grin and bear it whilst I sang them myself. For young children I have found the songs easiest to sing along to in French toy departments in the 'Jardin des Chansons' series, unfortunately not to be found over here.

Overtaken by 'teacher's doom'

For the prestige of the department, a foreign language carol seems essential for the Christmas service, particularly if parents are to be present. In French, this can be a problem as none of the traditional carols are ideal. I have had good results with only three: 'Il est né, le divin enfant', 'Douce Nuit' and 'Mon Beau Sapin'. Even with these, modifications have to be carried out if your singers are of less than choirboy standard. My voice is perfectly suited to carrying out those modifications (it's called 'enabling'). For example, no way would Year 5 get to sing, carrying onto the stage their wondrously decorated Christmas tree cut-outs, were it not for my carefully crafted *croakers' version* of 'Mon Beau Sapin', with it's vast range. But there is more to presenting a successful carol than simply singing it well. You must plan for every eventuality:

(1) Best results come from coaching one single class to a very high standard.
(2) but for maximum glory, do a whole-school carol. The results will be more ragged, but it is far more impressive as an event. (The parents think they can hear *their* child singing). There will also be a high rate of ML staff absence the following day (exhaustion).
(3) Do not rely on any help which may have been promised from the music department in terms of final rehearsals etc. (On the day they will be far too busy panicking).
(4) When the day arrives it is always possible that you will be overtaken by 'teacher's doom'. Every teacher of more than six weeks knows what this is. It recurs with monotonous regularity throughout our working lives, hangs over our heads like the sword of Damocles, gives us sleepless nights and palpitations, makes us bad-tempered at home and ages us before our time. What is this terrible scourge? (If any teacher reading this book tells you they have never suffered, don't believe them). It is not the fear of losing the A-level papers, locking the Chairman of Governors in the loo overnight, having one of your group elope during an exchange visit or accidentally burning the school down. It is the fear of *Not Being Ready*! (Not Being Ready for the inspectors' visit, your class assembly, sports day, your play performance, open evening, or the hundred and one events which depend on your ability, and yours alone, to organise the carefree irresponsibility of youth into an interesting and presentable performance).

'Highly Efficient Teacher Status'

For the normal teacher, it is difficult to be philosophical about Not Being Ready. I'm not sure why this should be so. After all, on one's death-bed one is unlikely to remember the relay team who ran the wrong way round the track, or the audience laughing at the French carol. And what does it matter if the cast fails to turn up for your assembly, or perform so ignominiously that no-one can hear them? So why do these insignificant events in the life of your average teacher cause more stress than moving house or losing one's job? In my own case, I think it is something to do with fear of losing face, that is, my status as 'Highly Efficient Teacher'. ('H.E.T.S' must be the next step up after 'B.A.Q.T.S!) The truth is that in a long teaching career I remember only episode of Not Being Ready which really was as cataclysmic as I had feared it might be.

'Mutiny on the buses'

If you have ever worked in a country comprehensive where almost all pupils are brought in by bus from surrounding small towns and villages, you will be aware of that greatest taboo of all, which is 'Not Being Ready for the Buses'. These buses have to leave at the appointed time because they have other engagements at other schools etc. later on in the afternoon. If the whole school is not assembled ready to go when they arrive, truculent drivers get out of their cabs, come into the school and make threats. The most dire threat of all – which leaves every adult in school in fear and trembling (and not just teachers) – is that they will leave in five minutes, *with or without* children! At four o'clock on a Friday afternoon, what could strike more fear into a teacher's heart? This partic-ular Friday was the last riotous day of the summer term. After all the junketing, the last hour had been dedicated, as usual, to tidying up our class-rooms. A new item had been added to the agenda this year, and that was: *cleaning our display boards*. What is more, the Head had made one of those decrees which high office and end of term euphoria sometimes result in: no-one was to leave until *every* classroom, and especially every board, had been satisfactorily inspected and declared clean by the Deputy Head. My class was at the very top of a huge sprawling building, so he arrived with us last of all. Below us, every other class in the school had been satisfactoriy inspected and was milling about, raring to go. But much to our surprise, we failed our inspection. We had put in a lot of effort with our battered old display boards, about which I had complained more than once, but we failed. Cleaning fluid and elbow grease had been applied. But our boards were found wanting. We couldn't believe it. Despite the pres-sures of the situation, the Deputy Head and I could not come to an agreement on this. He handed me the cleaning bottle, I handed it back. We both waited. The class watched, awestruck. It was far more exciting than the confrontation in 'High Noon'. A vast fleet of buses had by now arrived and were sounding their horns at the front of the school. Over a thousand pupils were by now massed in the forecourt, churning with the excite-ment that only the last day of the last term of the year can bring. The Head himself was on the tannoy summoning 'class 6JP, please' increasingly wildly. Bus drivers were beginning to climb out of their cabs. Emissaries were sent to my room. The tannoy was becoming more and more agitated: 'Is class 6JP ready please?', 'Will class 6JP come down to the front of the school *now*', 'Is class 6JP ready please?' We Were *Not Ready*, and what is more, there was no way we were going to *Be Ready* either. The Deputy and I were too entrenched in our positions to move now: the poor Head never stood a chance. He toiled up the stairs to intervene, understood without even looking at the offending boards that all was lost, and gave us permission to go. (Over the holiday, every display board in the school was freshly painted!). Forward planning is essential, but it is not infallible, and if it should happen to you at Christmas, do not fear, just take advantage of my experience, place a copy of the words on the chair of every person in the hall, including parents, staff, visitors and headteacher, and do 'Douce Nuit'. At least they all know the tune!

'Ten green bottles' or 'Frère Jacques'?

Every teacher will have their own approach to songs, and an infinite variety of objectives in their use. Many are specially written to accompany coursebooks, with the intention of consolidating vocabulary etc. Some colleagues enjoy concocting lyrics to English songs for the same purpose, and very intriguing and entertaining they are. I have experimented with many classes with all of these, and have come to the reluctant conclusion that, whilst they are ingenious, such songs, especially those cobbled together for grammar purposes, are not half as effective, or half as much fun, as the traditional French songs sung by children down the ages. (With the exception of the very popular 'Comptons jusqu'a dix' from 'Primary French' – always a big hit with beginners). They just do not get the children singing with the same flair and enthusiasm. I imagine the same thing applies in all languages. Traditional songs have not lasted down the centuries for no reason. They have a special appeal, an appeal which children recognise to this day, and they lend themselves perfectly to active participation.

Make it a very large pillow

For your first lesson (especially if you can't sing at all), 'Frère Jacques' is an excellent starter because:

(1) it is easy for the teacher to sing (no high notes);
(2) it lends itself to simple actions;
(3) It can be done in rounds, and children love rounds.

Have as many rounds as you like, building up slowly. The children will be enthusiastic about this, because they will be competing with other classes as to who can sing in the most parts. 'F. J' is also useful for performances in assembly or, along with others, in a middle school concert of French songs given by Year 5 for the new intake. Each song must be accompanied by a comical scene. For example, have a sleeping monk being woken by someone beating him over the head with a large pillow. For some reason, young children find the pillow irresistible.

The boy who would rather pick his nose

Moving on from here you have probably the best choice of material for performance that you will ever have e.g. 'Sur le pont d'Avignon', easy to sing and can be done with actions, standing behind desks, or actual dancing if you have room in your classroom, or for a performance. Make the songs as active as you can at this stage. Using music to help language acquisition has been recognised for many years as part of the 'multisensory approach' to learning (*'Language Learning Journal'*, 1994). Using movement and emotion has been found to stimulate the affective and creative hemisphere of the brain, and improve short-term memory. (I would be surprised if it did not improve long-term memory as well.) Another reason to incorporate actions into your songs, is that they keep everyone busy, especially the hyperactive boy who would rather pick his nose. Very few actions are needed to be effective. If your song is very active indeed (e.g. 'Savez-vous planter des choux'), have one individual in turn acting the whole thing out at the front, whilst the rest of the class do a modified (*very* modified) version in their seats.

With a song in their hearts

A much-loved song is an opportunity for relaxation, repetition, memorisation, mastery and pleasure. Go with the enthusiasm of the group and don't make the song into a gap-fill or some sort of listening/reading test. Songs certainly lend themselves to this approach. You could even replace all the words with grammar structures if you liked. But why make a wonderful opportunity for getting into the spirit of a country and getting closer to the culture you are learning about into just another grammar lesson? A song will only represent an opportunity for relaxation, repetition, memorisation, mastery, and pleasure if the singers love it. It has to be sung so many times to achieve its purpose. And because of its multisensory quality, the language (including all its grammar points) will be remembered and available for re-use for a very long time indeed. The 'grammar' will take care of itself. Any teenager learning to sing 'Les feuilles mortes', for example:

'C'est une chanson qui nous ressemble
Toi, qui m'aimais, moi, qui t'aimais.
Nous vivions tous les deux ensemble
Toi, qui m'aimais, moi, qui t'aimais
Mais la vie sépare ceux qui s'aiment
Tout doucement sans faire de bruit
Et la mer efface sur le sable, les pas des amants désunis'

will pick up not only beautiful pronunciation of some difficult words, but understanding of the use of the Imperfect tense, the tricky constructions 'ceux qui' and 'sans faire de', plus lots of useful vocabulary, without even realising it.

Gags all round for the first few listenings

However enthusiastic the group and however keen to get started, it is impossible for them to plunge into singing a new song straight away. Whilst no-one wants a class to associate learning a song with tedium, a certain few preparatory steps must be taken:

(1) they must hear it more than once;
(2) they must have some idea of what the words mean;
(3) they must be able to make a reasonable stab at pronunciation.

I usually start with a quick translation of the words on the OHP, so that they know what they are singing about. A class will not sing well words they do not understand. Participation by the class in that initial translation is welcome, as long as it is quick, but it is not required. (They will usually leap to fill in the easy parts, whether you want them to or not). This part of the process should not take too long, because it is not the point of the exercise.

Be boring and irritating, but be brief

Several listenings then follow. The words are available on OHP but only for those who wish to follow them. Some will make better use of an auditory rather than a visual stimulus. No-one is allowed to join in yet. Never ask learners to join in with a song they have not heard several times, however keen they are to start. The more they hear it, the more they will want to join in, and the better the first attempt will be. You are aiming at a success situation. Nothing is more discouraging than failing to keep up with a song. Have them repeat the words after you first, but probably not all of them, depending on difficulty. Repeating words after teacher is one of the most boring and irritating activities known to man, so do it only the moment before they *know* they are about to sing, when they are motivated. Choose lines within their scope to begin with, perhaps the chorus or one or two lines only if they are young learners or have difficulty. It could even be one word only. Better to sing only 'Vive le vent!' competently than to make a mess of the whole of 'Jingle Bells'. They will naturally branch out to cover more and more of the words as they repeat the song each lesson and gain confidence. If your class is never going to master the whole thing, divide them into groups singing one or two lines each, and in this way they can have the satisfaction of singing the whole song. Helping with other groups' lines is fine.

Pick of the pops

There is a song for every age group and every level of difficulty. Advanced students who go to France will sometimes bring in their own treasures, which can be fun, although some are quite indecipherable to the more mature ear of the teacher. If a French song should suddenly become a hit over here of course it is a must, but this is not something that happens every day. ('Joe le taxi' was one such). The following are popular and fun to perform: all the classics can be found in your local library's music section. 'Voyage, voyage' was brought in by a girl from a stay in France, and contains songs which are riveting not only musically, but by their particular challenge to pronunciation – keep your sixth-formers gasping.

Top ten (beginners)

(1) Frère Jacques (trad.)
(2) Sur le pont d'Avignon (trad.)
(3) Comptons jusqu'a dix (Primary French)
(4) Meunier, tu dors (trad.)
(5) Au clair de la lune (trad.)
(6) Alouette (trad.)
(7) Savez-vous planter les choux (trad.)
(8) Dans la forêt lointaine (trad.) (the 'coucou' song'!)
(9) Fais dodo (trad.)
(10) Dites-moi pourquoi la vie est belle. (South Pacific)

Top ten (enthusiasts)

(1) A la volette (trad.)
(2) Dominique (Soeur Sourire)
(3) Douce France (Charles Trenet)
(4) Avec mes sabots (trad.)
(5) Joe le taxi (Vanessa Paradis)
(6) La mer (Charles Trenet)
(7) Ne pleure pas Jeanette (trad.)
(8) Marjolaine (trad.)
(9) Chevaliers de la table ronde (trad.)
(10) la Marseillaise (Rouget de Lisle)

Top ten (Sixth Form)

(1) Cheminant dans la ville (McGarrigle sisters)
(2) Les feuilles mortes (Yves Montand)
(3) Brave Margot (Georges Brassens)
(4) Boum! (Charles Trenet)
(5) Exodus (Edith Piaf)
(6) Milord (Edith Piaf)
(7) Valentine (Maurice Chevalier)
(8) Les amoureux qui tricotent sur les bancs publics (Georges Brassens)
(9) Voyage, voyage (Desireless)
(10) La cigale et la fourmi (Charles Trenet)

Douce nuit, Sainte nuit

Douce nuit, sainte nuit,
Dans les cieux, l'astre reluit,
Le message annonce s'accomplit.
Cet enfant sur la paille dormit.
C'est l'Amour Infini!
C'est l'Amour Infini!